INSIGHTS TO LITERATURE

by Judith Cochran

Incentive Publications, Inc.
Nashville, Tennessee

*Dedicated to my parents who believed
in the importance of literature and who read to me often.*

Cover and illustrations by Susan Eaddy

ISBN 0-86530-142-5

Table of Contents

My Side Of The Mountain

Bridge To Terabithia

A Wrinkle In Time

Island Of The Blue Dolphins

HOW TO USE THIS BOOK

INSIGHTS TO LITERATURE is a complete reading program designed to accompany ten widely acclaimed books for grades 4 - 8. Utilizing a whole language and thematic approach to teaching literature, this book ensures a higher range of comprehension, skills development, and appreciation for great literature.

Each piece of literature referenced in this book is presented through an Individual Learning Unit and a Teacher's Guide. Every Individual Learning Unit contains comprehension questions/activities for each chapter of the book, Journal writing activities that relate to the story and the students' own experiences (reproduce the journal entry form on page ix in quantities to meet the needs of the class), and culminating project activities. All of the materials in the Individual Learning Units may be reproduced to meet the needs of the class.

Every Teacher's Guide contains pre/post reading questions/activities which link the students' experiences to the story and touch upon all areas of the curriculum, journal writing activities, and thematic activities for math, science, social studies, and fine arts. Also included are instructions for completing a "story frame" or book summary for the specific title (reproduce the story frame on page x in quantities to meet the needs of the class). "Chain the responses" in the Teacher's Guide should be done as follows:

Ev How would these chapters have been different if the rats hadn't learned to read? ("Chain" student responses.)

EXAMPLE:

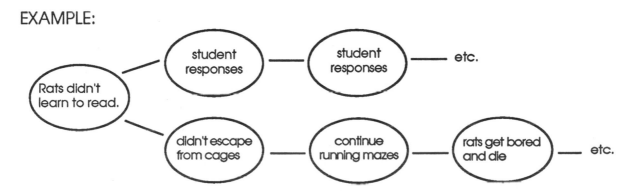

All of the questions and activities in the Individual Learning Units and Teacher's Guides are correlated to Bloom's Taxonomy with a particular emphasis on the upper levels requiring critical thinking. Each question and activity is marked with an abbreviation denoting the specific level it reinforces:

K	=	Knowledge
C	=	Comprehension
Ap	=	Application
An	=	Analysis
Sy	=	Synthesis
Ev	=	Evaluation

INSIGHTS TO LITERATURE can be easily implemented in any classroom and can be used as a total reading program or can serve as a supplement to any other program already in use. It can be utilized with a whole group, small group, or even individual students. Depending upon the ability level of the group, the program works equally well whether the teacher reads the book to the students, directs reading in reading groups, assigns the reading as homework, or uses any combination of these methods.

With interest in literature on the rise, well-rounded reading/literature programs are sorely needed. INSIGHTS TO LITERATURE meets this need by offering a comprehensive program based on the latest research with an excellent balance between skills, critical thinking, and literacy appreciation that fits easily into any intermediate classroom.

JOURNAL

STORY FRAME

Do this with your teacher.

CHARACTERS	SETTING	SUMMARY

The Velveteen Rabbit

THE VELVETEEN RABBIT

K 1. Who is the author of this book? _____

K 2. To whom is the book dedicated?_____

Rewrite sentences 3 - 6 on another piece of paper. Look up the underlined words in the dictionary.

C 3. There once was a <u>velveteen</u> rabbit.

C 4. He was really <u>splendid</u>.

C 5. They unwrapped <u>parcels</u>.

K 6. What time of year was it? _____

An 7. On another piece of paper, draw a picture of the Velveteen Rabbit. Describe him.

K 8. On another piece of paper, draw the other things that were in the stocking with the rabbit and label each item.

Ev 9. Why do you think the mechanical toys looked down on the Velveteen Rabbit?

_____

K 10. Did the Velveteen Rabbit know that *real* rabbits exist? _____

What did he think real rabbits were made of? _____

C 11. What was the only toy that was kind to the Velveteen Rabbit?_____

An 12. Describe the Skin Horse. _____

K 13. What did the Skin Horse say about becoming real? _____

_____

K 14. Does being real hurt? Explain. _____

_____

K 15. What did the Velveteen Rabbit want more than anything? _____

_____

K 16. How did the Velveteen Rabbit get to sleep with the boy? _____

_____

Rewrite sentences 17 - 19 on another piece of paper. Look up the underlined words in the dictionary.

C   **17.** He pushed him so far under the pillows that the rabbit could <u>scarcely</u> breathe.

C   **18.** He said they were like <u>burrows</u> in which the real rabbits live.

C   **19.** Nana had left the night-light burning on the <u>mantelpiece</u>.

Ev   **20.** On another piece of paper, draw a picture of what you think the Velveteen Rabbit dreamed of when he slept with the boy. Explain your picture.

C   **21.** What was happening to the rabbit when he was so happy with the boy?

_____

An   **22.** On another piece of paper, draw the three things the boy would do for the rabbit in the spring. Label each picture.

Ap   **23.** When the boy said the Velveteen Rabbit was real, how do you think the rabbit felt? _____

_____

On another piece of paper, rewrite sentences 24 - 26. Look up the underlined words in the dictionary.

C   **24.** The boy would play at <u>brigands</u> under the tree.

C   **25.** The boy made a nest for the rabbit among the <u>bracken</u>.

C   **26.** The rabbit tried to see out of which side the <u>clockwork</u> hung.

An   **27.** On another piece of paper, list three ways the Velveteen Rabbit and a real rabbit are the same and three ways they are different.

Ev   **28.** Why do you think the Velveteen Rabbit told the real rabbits that he could jump? _____

_____

C   **29.** What did the Velveteen Rabbit mean when he said, "I *am* real!" _____

_____

C   **30.** What does this mean: "He loved him so hard that he loved all the whiskers off"?

_____

Ev 31. Although the rabbit found it dull when the boy was ill, he snuggled down patiently with the boy. Why? _____

_____

Ap 32. If you were the rabbit, what delightful things would you have whispered in the boy's ear? Draw and describe these things on another piece of paper.

Rewrite sentences 33 - 36 on another piece of paper. Look up the underlined words in the dictionary.

C 33. His face grew very <u>flushed</u> and he talked in his sleep.

C 34. When you are real, <u>shabbiness</u> doesn't matter.

C 35. It was a long, <u>weary</u> time.

C 36. The room was to be <u>disinfected</u>.

C 37. On another piece of paper, draw what the boy wanted to see at the seaside and describe each thing.

C 38. What is a fowl-house? _____

Ap 39. What would you have done to keep the boy and the rabbit together after the boy was well? _____

_____

An 40. On another piece of paper, list the kinds of rubbish you think might have been in the sack with the Velveteen Rabbit.

Sy 41. The rabbit thought of his time with the boy and a great sadness came over him. Describe a time when a great sadness came over you. _____

_____

An 42. On another piece of paper, draw a picture of the mysterious flower.

Ap 43. On another piece of paper, draw and describe a toy that you have loved so much that it might have become real.

An 44. Write a new title for the book and explain it. _____

_____

An 45. On another piece of paper, draw and label pictures of the five main events of the story in the order that they occurred.

Sy 46. Write a summary of the book on another piece of paper.

THE VELVETEEN RABBIT

1. Sew your own velveteen rabbit.

2. Make a diorama to illustrate part of the story.

3. Conduct research about rabbits and write a two-page report giving your findings.

4. Make a picture book to illustrate the different toys mentioned in the book. Label each picture.

5. Write a story about your favorite toy becoming real.

6. Perform a puppet show to tell the story.

7. Interview three people who have read *The Velveteen Rabbit*. Write a newspaper article about their responses to the story.

8. Advertise the book by tape-recording a commercial and designing a billboard or magazine ad.

THE VELVETEEN RABBIT

PRELIMINARY ACTIVITIES

GETTING READY TO READ:

C   What is *velveteen?*   *a cotton cloth with short, thick pile, resembling velvet*

K   Who is the author?   *Margery Williams*

Ap   Where do you think the story takes place?   *answers will vary*

Ap   How many characters might there be?   *answers will vary*

An   What do you think the story is about?   *answers will vary*

PREREADING DISCUSSION:

An   How is being real different from being imaginary?

JOURNAL WRITING: Discussion; Students Write

An   What kinds of things can a real thing do that imaginary things can't do?

FIRST SECTION (Individual Learning Unit #1-#23)

VOCABULARY:

C

burrows	disabled	scarcely	sprig
clockwork	mantelpiece	shabby	swagger
commonplace	parcel	splendid	technical

PREREADING DISCUSSION:

C   What has happened to a toy that you have loved a lot? How can you tell that the toy was "used"? Read to find out what this author has to say about what happens to the toys that are loved the most.

THE VELVETEEN RABBIT

POSTREADING: Teacher Reads; Discussion; Teacher Writes On Board

Read aloud the passage beginning, "It doesn't happen all at once," and ending with, "...you can't be ugly, except to people who don't understand."

An What kinds of toys do you think can become real and what kinds of toys can't become real?

JOURNAL WRITING: Teacher Reads; Students Write

"For nursery magic is very strange and wonderful and only those playthings that are old and wise and experienced like the Skin Horse understand all about it."

An Did you have a toy that was similar to the Skin Horse? Explain the similarities.

SECOND SECTION (Individual Learning Unit #24-#30)

Begins: "That was a wonderful summer!"

VOCABULARY:

C bracken   brigands   cosy   dreadful

PREREADING DISCUSSION:

Ev Do you think the Velveteen Rabbit is really real? Why or why not? Read to find out whether or not you are right.

POSTREADING DISCUSSION:

An How was the Velveteen Rabbit different from the real rabbits?

Ev Do you think Velveteen Rabbit realized that he wasn't really real? Why or why not?

JOURNAL WRITING: Students Write

Ev Imagine that you are one of the real rabbits. Write about your feelings and your experience with the Velveteen Rabbit.

THE VELVETEEN RABBIT

LAST SECTION (Individual Learning Unit #31 -#45)

Begins: "Weeks passed and the little Rabbit grew very old and shabby."

VOCABULARY:

C

bedclothes	emeralds	nonsense	thicket
dingy	fronds	patient	threadbare
disinfected	mysterious	rubbish	turf

PREREADING DISCUSSION:

An How can you help a loved one who is sick? Read to find out what the Velveteen Rabbit does.

POSTREADING DISCUSSION:

Ev How do you think the Velveteen Rabbit felt being real? How do you think he felt about leaving the boy?

JOURNAL WRITING: Students Write

Sy Imagine that you are the Velveteen Rabbit and write a letter to the boy describing what it is like being real.

CULMINATING ACTIVITIES

POSTREADING DISCUSSION:

What kinds of things do you think the Velveteen Rabbit had to learn about Rabbitland?

STORY FRAME: Discussion; Students Read; Teacher Writes On Board; Students Fill In Story Frames

 Have the students fill in the characters and setting on their story frames. Discuss the plot and then have the students review their chapter summaries. Ask the class to brainstorm major events in the story (list these on the board). Consolidate statements and ideas until everyone has an understanding of the summary. Then have the students fill in the summary sections of their story frames.

JOURNAL WRITING: Students Write

 Have each student choose one of the following culminating activities:

- Write about the Velveteen Rabbit's life after he went to live with the real rabbits.

- What happened to the boy after he lost the Velveteen Rabbit?

- Write a newspaper article about the nursery magic that changed a toy into a real thing.

- Write a diary of the Velveteen Rabbit's experiences.

THE VELVETEEN RABBIT

MATH

GRAPHING/MEASURING:

Have the students bring stuffed toys to class and categorize the toys according to the kind of animal, the color, and the shape. Help the students graph the results. Then have the students measure the height, width, and circumference of each toy and graph these results as well.

SOCIAL STUDIES

COMPARATIVE STUDIES:

Discuss the life-style changes that the Velveteen Rabbit would have to make in order to live like a real rabbit. Ask the students to compare the Velveteen Rabbit's life as a real rabbit with his life as a stuffed toy.

SCIENCE

RABBITS:

Have the students study the life cycle of the rabbit and compare it to the "life" of a stuffed rabbit.

FINE ARTS

SEWING:

Have the students make their own stuffed animals using buttons for eyes and embroidering for other features.

PUPPETS:

Have the students create puppets to represent the characters in the book and then reenact the story.

Charlotte's Web

CHARLOTTE'S WEB

1. Who is the author of this book?_____

K **2.** To whom is the book dedicated?_____

K **3.** Name another book this author has written._____

K **4.** How many chapters does this book have?_____

CHAPTER 1—BEFORE BREAKFAST

Rewrite sentences 5 - 7 on another piece of paper. Look up the underlined words in the dictionary.

C **5.** A <u>weakling</u> makes trouble.

C **6.** This is the most terrible case of <u>injustice</u> I have ever heard.

C **7.** That's a fine <u>specimen</u> of a pig.

Ev **8.** On another piece of paper, tell why you think a weakling might make trouble.

Ap **9.** On another piece of paper, draw and label the smells of the kitchen.

K **10.** On another piece of paper, list the characters in this chapter.

Ev **11.** What other name would you give the pig? _____

_____

Sy **12.** What different title would you give this chapter and why? _____

_____

An **13.** On another piece of paper, draw pictures of the three main events in this chapter and label them in order.

CHAPTER 2—WILBUR

Rewrite sentences 14 - 16 on another piece of paper. Look up the underlined words in the dictionary.

C **14.** He would stand and <u>gaze</u> up at her with adoring eyes.

C **15.** Fern was <u>enchanted</u>.

CHARLOTTE'S WEB

C   **16.** Wilbur's <u>appetite</u> had increased.

C   **17.** On another piece of paper, list the words used in the book to describe the mud along the edge of the brook. Then list your own descriptive words.

C   **18.** Wilbur was a *spring pig.* On another piece of paper, explain what this means.

C   **19.** On another piece of paper, describe a time when you had to sell or give away something you loved very much.

Sy   **20.** What different title would you give this chapter and why? _____

_____

An   **21.** On another piece of paper, draw pictures of the three main events in this chapter and label them in order.

CHAPTER 3—ESCAPE

Rewrite sentences 22 - 24 on another piece of paper. Look up the underlined words in the dictionary.

C   **22.** It smelled of the <u>perspiration</u> of tired horses.

C   **23.** She found an old milking stool that had been <u>discarded</u>.

C   **24.** He walked slowly to his food <u>trough</u>.

K   **25.** Which animal told Wilbur to get loose? _____

Ev   **26.** Where would you have gone if you were Wilbur and had escaped from your pen? Why? _____

_____

_____

C   **27.** On another piece of paper, list the animals mentioned in this chapter.

Sy   **28.** What different title would you give this chapter and why? _____

_____

_____

An   **29.** On another piece of paper, draw pictures of the three main events In this chapter and label them in order.

CHARLOTTE'S WEB

CHAPTER 4 —LONELINESS

Rewrite sentences 30 - 32 on another piece of paper. Look up the underlined words in the dictionary.

C 30. The rain dripped <u>steadily</u> from the <u>eaves</u>.

C 31. Talking to Templeton was not the most interesting <u>occupation</u>.

C 32. For a while he stood <u>gloomily</u> indoors.

C 33. On another piece of paper, list the plans Wilbur had for the day.

C 34. Who is Templeton? _____

_____

K 35. What is a glutton? _____

_____

K 36. What medicine was given to Wilbur? _____

_____

An 37. On another piece of paper, draw pictures of the three main events in this chapter and label them in order.

CHAPTER 5—CHARLOTTE

Rewrite sentences 38 - 40 on another piece of paper. Look up the underlined words in the dictionary.

C 38. Templeton had quit working and had gone somewhere on an <u>errand</u>.

C 39. Why can't he go to sleep like any <u>decent</u> animal?

C 40. <u>Salutations</u>!

K 41. How long does it take a goose egg to be hatched? _____

_____

C 42. What does the goose do with her eggs when she goes for a walk?_____

_____

CHARLOTTE'S WEB

Ap 43. Write three salutations on another piece of paper.

C 44. Why can't Charlotte see Wilbur very well? _____

_____

K 45. On another piece of paper, list the things that Charlotte eats.

K 46. What does Charlotte do rather than eat the bugs? _____

_____

C 47. What is going to happen to Wilbur at Christmas? _____

_____

Sy 48. What different title would you give this chapter and why? _____

_____

An 49. On another piece of paper, draw pictures of the three main events in this chapter and label them in order.

CHAPTER 6—SUMMER DAYS

Rewrite sentences 50 - 52 on another piece of paper. Look up the underlined words in the dictionary.

C 50. The hay would be <u>hoisted</u> into the big loft.

C 51. Early summer days are a <u>jubilee</u> time for birds.

C 52. She knew they were most <u>anxious</u> to break through and escape.

K 53. On another piece of paper, list the birds mentioned and their calls.

Ev 54. On another piece of paper, list the unusual objects Templeton collected.

K 55. Why were the goose and gander worried about Templeton? _____

_____

Sy 56. What different title would you give this chapter and why? _____

_____

An 57. On another piece of paper, draw pictures of the three main events in this chapter and label them in order.

CHARLOTTE'S WEB

CHAPTER 7—BAD NEWS

Rewrite sentences 58 - 60 on another piece of paper. Look up the underlined words in the dictionary.

C   **58.** Fern grew <u>rigid</u> on her stool.

C   **59.** Her <u>campaign</u> against insects was sensible and useful.

C   **60.** I can't stand <u>hysterics</u>.

K   **61.** Who told Wilbur he was going to be killed? _____

_____

Ev   **62.** If you were Wilbur, what things would you miss and why? _____

_____

Sy   **63.** What different title would you give this chapter and why? _____

_____

An   **64.** On another piece of paper, draw pictures of the three main events in this chapter and label them in order.

CHAPTER 8—A TALK AT HOME

C   **65.** On another piece of paper, write Charlotte's speech.

Sy   **66.** How could Fern have kept her parents from worrying? _____

_____

Sy   **67.** What different title would you give this chapter and why? _____

_____

An   **68.** What is the main thing that happens in this chapter? _____

_____

CHAPTER 9—WILBUR'S BOAST

Rewrite sentences 69 - 71 on another piece of paper. Look up the underlined words in the dictionary.

C   **69.** A spider's web is made of thin, <u>delicate</u> strands.

C   **70.** He glanced <u>hastily</u> behind himself.

CHARLOTTE'S WEB

C 71. Anything to <u>oblige</u>.

K 72. When did Charlotte like to repair her web? _____

K 73. List the seven sections of a spider's leg on another piece of paper.

C 74. What did Wilbur say he could do? _____

C 75. List three things Charlotte told Wilbur to do to help her save his life. _____

_____

Sy 76. What different title would you give this chapter and why? _____

_____

An 77. On another piece of paper, draw pictures of the three main events in this chapter and label them in order.

CHAPTER 10—AN EXPLOSION

Rewrite sentences 78 - 80 on another piece of paper. Look up the underlined words in the dictionary.

C 78. Charlotte was naturally <u>patient</u>.

C 79. The spider gazed <u>affectionately</u> at him.

C 80. Then you <u>straddled</u> the knot.

K 81. On another piece of paper, tell what Avery tried to do at Wilbur's pigpen.

K 82. What happened to Avery? _____

_____

K 83. What made Fern and Avery leave? _____

_____

Sy 84. What different title would you give this chapter and why? _____

_____

CHAPTER 11—THE MIRACLE

Rewrite sentences 85 - 87 on another piece of paper. Look up the underlined words in the dictionary.

C 85. The web <u>glistened</u> in the light.

CHARLOTTE'S WEB

C 86. He dropped to his knees and <u>uttered</u> a short prayer.

C 87. He walked <u>solemnly</u> back to the house.

K 88. On another piece of paper, tell what Mr. Zuckerman thought about the web.

Ev 89. On another piece of paper, tell how you think Wilbur is unusual.

C 90. List three things that changed after everyone thought Wilbur was "some pig."

_____

Sy 91. What different title would you give this chapter and why? _____

_____

An 92. On another piece of paper, draw pictures of the three main events in this chapter and label them in order.

CHAPTER 12—A MEETING

Rewrite sentences 93 - 95 on another piece of paper. Look up the underlined words in the dictionary.

C 93. I guess we can <u>proceed</u> without him.

C 94. He saw the animals <u>assembled</u>.

C 95. I think you're <u>sensational</u>.

K 96. Why did Charlotte call the meeting? _____

_____

C 97. On another piece of paper, explain what this statement means: "People believe almost anything they see in print."

C 98. Why does Templeton agree to help? _____

_____

K 99. What word will Charlotte write in her web and whose idea was it? _____

_____

Sy 100. What different title would you give this chapter and why? _____

_____

CHARLOTTE'S WEB

C   **101.** On another piece of paper, draw pictures of the three main events in this chapter and label them in order.

CHAPTER 13—GOOD PROGRESS

Ev   Rewrite sentences 102 - 104 on another piece of paper. Look up the underlined words in the dictionary.

C   **102.** A spider can <u>produce</u> several kinds of thread.

C   **103.** She climbed up and made another <u>attachment</u>.

C   **104.** Tired from his <u>romp</u>, Wilbur lay down.

K   **105.** What two kinds of threads can a spider produce? _____

_____

K   **106.** List the three advertisement words that Templeton brought. _____

_____

C   **107.** What did Wilbur think of the straw in his pen? _____

_____

Sy   **108.** On another piece of paper, write a story that Charlotte might tell.

Sy   **109.** What different title would you give this chapter and why? _____

_____

An   **110.** On another piece of paper, write three sentences to describe the main events in this chapter.

CHAPTER 14—DR. DORIAN

Rewrite sentences 111 - 113 on another piece of paper. Look up the underlined words in the dictionary.

C   **111.** You must not <u>invent</u> things.

C   **112.** The fist got <u>tangled</u> in the web.

C   **113.** It is a very <u>sociable</u> place.

C   **114.** Why did Mrs. Arable visit the doctor? _____

_____

CHARLOTTE'S WEB

Sy   **115.** What different title would you give this chapter and why? _____

_____

An   **116.** On another piece of paper, write three sentences to describe the main events in this chapter.

CHAPTER 15—THE CRICKETS

Rewrite sentences 117 - 119 on another piece of paper. Look up the underlined words in the dictionary.

C   **117.** The crickets spread the <u>rumor</u> of sadness and change.

C   **118.** I shall find it <u>inconvenient</u> to leave home.

C   **119.** If he could <u>distinguish</u> himself at the fair, Mr. Zuckerman would let him live.

K   **120.** Who warns everyone that summertime is ending? _____

K   **121.** What was Wilbur's bad dream? _____

_____

C   **122.** What was Charlotte getting ready to do? _____

_____

Sy   **123.** What different title would you give this chapter and why? _____

_____

An   **124.** On another piece of paper, write three sentences to describe the main events in this chapter.

CHAPTER 16—OFF TO THE FAIR

Rewrite sentences 125 - 127 on another piece of paper. Look up the underlined words in the dictionary.

C   **125.** He also has a <u>smudge</u> where he lays in the manure.

C   **126.** Charlotte had her web looking fine for the <u>occasion</u>.

C   **127.** He could feel the buttermilk <u>trickling</u> down his sides.

C   **128.** With what did Mrs. Zuckerman bathe Wilbur? _____

CHARLOTTE'S WEB

An 129. After his bath, Wilbur was "smooth as silk." On another piece of paper, list other things things that are "smooth as silk."

C 130. What did Mr. Arable say that made Wilbur feel faint? _____

_____

Sy 131. What different title would you give this chapter and why? _____

_____

An 132. On another piece of paper, write three sentences to describe the main events in this chapter.

CHAPTER 17—UNCLE

Rewrite sentences 133 - 135 on another piece of paper. Look up the underlined words in the dictionary.

C 133. They could smell the dust of the race track where the sprinkling cart had <u>molstened</u> it.

C 134. An <u>enormous</u> voice came over the loudspeaker.

C 135. Charlotte <u>ascended</u> slowly and returned to Wilbur's pen.

C 136. On another piece of paper, write what the following characters wanted to see or do at the fair: Fern and Avery, Mr. and Mrs. Zuckerman, and Lurvy.

C 137. Charlotte "seemed listless." What was wrong with her? _____

_____

Ev 138. Who do you think will win the pig contest, Wilbur or Uncle? Why? _____

_____

Sy 139. What different title would you give this chapter and why? _____

_____

An 140. On another piece of paper, write three sentences to describe the main events in this chapter.

CHAPTER 18—THE COOL OF THE EVENING

Rewrite sentences 141 - 143 on another piece of paper. Look up the underlined words in the dictionary.

CHARLOTTE'S WEB

C   **141.** The evening came as a welcome <u>relief</u> to all.

C   **142.** Templeton's nose <u>detected</u> many fine smells in the air.

C   **143.** I'm not going to spend all of my time <u>fetching</u> and carrying.

C   **144.** On another piece of paper, describe what each of these characters was doing at the beginning of the chapter: Templeton, Wilbur, Charlotte.

K   **145.** What did Charlotte ask Templeton to bring? Why? _____

_____

K   **146.** What did Fern say when her mother asked her if she had a good time? ____

_____

Sy   **147.** What different title would you give this chapter and why? _____

_____

An   **148.** On another piece of paper, write three sentences to describe the main events in this chapter.

CHAPTER 19—THE EGG SAC

Rewrite sentences 149 - 151 on another piece of paper. Look up the underlined words in the dictionary.

C   **149.** I can <u>guarantee</u> that it is strong.

C   **150.** The rat eyed the sac <u>suspiciously</u>.

C   **151.** It would serve you right if you had an <u>acute</u> attack of indigestion.

K   **152.** What had Charlotte made? _____

C   **153.** Write the definition of "magnum opus" on another piece of paper.

Ev   **154.** What is Charlotte's problem? _____

_____

Ap   **155.** On another piece of paper, draw Charlotte's web in the dew.

Sy   **156.** What different title would you give this chapter and why?_____

_____

CHARLOTTE'S WEB

An **157.** On another piece of paper, write three sentences to describe the main events in this chapter.

CHAPTER 20—THE HOUR OF TRIUMPH

Rewrite sentences 158 - 160 on another piece of paper. Look up the underlined words in the dictionary.

C **158.** Wilbur <u>trembled</u> when he heard this speech.

C **159.** The fame of the <u>unique</u> animal has spread to the corners of the earth.

C **160.** The pain <u>revived</u> Wilbur.

K **161.** What did Fern race off to do? _____

_____

K **162.** Will Fern see Wilbur get his award? _____

_____

K **163.** What kind of a prize did Wilbur win? _____

_____

K **164.** What did Wilbur do at the end of the announcer's speech? _____

_____

Sy **165.** What different title would you give this chapter and why? _____

_____

An **166.** On another piece of paper, write three sentences to describe the main events in this chapter.

CHAPTER 21—LAST DAY

Ev Rewrite sentences 167 - 169 on another piece of paper. Look up the underlined words in the dictionary.

C **167.** Wilbur lay resting after the <u>strain</u> of the ceremony.

C **168.** Your future is <u>assured</u>.

C **169.** She cannot <u>accompany</u> us home.

CHARLOTTE'S WEB

K 　**170.** Why did Charlotte say she helped Wilbur? _____

_____

K 　**171.** Why won't Charlotte be going back to the barn? _____

_____

Ev/An 　**172.** On another piece of paper, tell how Wilbur helped Charlotte.

K 　**173.** What did Wilbur promise Templeton if he would help? _____

_____

K 　**174.** How did Wilbur carry the egg sac? _____

_____

K 　**175.** How did Wilbur say good-bye? _____

_____

C 　**176.** What happened to Charlotte? _____

_____

Sy 　**177.** What different title would you give this chapter and why? _____

_____

An 　**178.** On another piece of paper, write three sentences to describe the main events in this chapter.

CHAPTER 22—A WARM WIND

Rewrite sentences 179 - 181 on another piece of paper. Look up the underlined words in the dictionary.

C 　**179.** He was <u>gigantic</u>.

C 　**180.** He walked <u>drearily</u> to the doorway.

C 　**181.** Many more <u>tranquil</u> days followed.

Ap 　**182.** On another piece of paper, draw a picture of Charlotte's torn, empty web.

C 　**183.** Did Wilbur keep his promise to Templeton? _____

CHARLOTTE'S WEB

1. Make a poster to advertise the book.

2. Write a report about spiders.

3. Visit a pig farm and tell about your visit.

4. Make a spider web with a "word" in it.

5. Make a diorama to illustrate part of the book.

6. Draw a picture of each animal in the story and write a sentence about each one. Compile the pictures to make a book.

7. Design a model of Templeton's rat house.

8. Cut words that describe Wilbur out of newspapers and magazines. Glue the pictures on poster board or heavy construction paper to make a collage.

9. Write a story about all of the things there are to do at a fair.

CHARLOTTE'S WEB

PRELIMINARY ACTIVITIES

GETTING READY TO READ:

K | Who is the author? *E.B. White*

K | Has the book won any awards? *Laura Ingalls Wilder Medal*

K | What other books has the author written? *Stuart Little, The Trumpet of the Swan*

Ap | How many characters might there be? *answers will vary*

An | What do you think the story is about? *answers will vary*

PREREADING DISCUSSION: Teacher Writes On Board

Ev | What kinds of things does a special friend do for you?

JOURNAL WRITING: Students Write

Sy | What kinds of things would you do for a special friend?

CHAPTER 1—Before Breakfast; CHAPTER 2—Wilbur

VOCABULARY:

C

adoring	carton	gaze	miserable	specimen
appetite	distribute	injustice	shrieked	vanish
blissful	enchanted	manure	sopping	weakling

PREREADING DISCUSSION:

Ev | Do you think it is right to kill the runt of a litter? Why?

An | What reasons for killing a runt do you think someone might have? Mr. Arable wants to kill the runt of the pig litter. Read to see what happens to his plan.

POSTREADING DISCUSSION: Students Skim Chapter 2; Teacher Writes On Board

An | Why does Mr. Arable want to sell Wilbur? Why does Fern want to keep him? Support the positions of Mr. Arable and Fern. (List the responses.)

JOURNAL WRITING: Students Write

Sy | Imagine that you are Fern. Write what you would say when you tell Wilbur good-bye. (Remind students to use quotation marks.)

CHARLOTTE'S WEB

CHAPTER 3—Escape; CHAPTER 4—Loneliness

VOCABULARY:

C

appealing	cunning	endure	goslings	relieved
cautious	discarded	frolic	patient	stealthily
commotion	eaves	gloomily	perspiration	trough

PREREADING DISCUSSION: Teacher Writes On Board

Ev Do you think Wilbur will like his new home? Why or why not?

An What do you think Wilbur will like and dislike about his new home?

POSTREADING DISCUSSION: Teacher Writes On Board

Ev How would things be different if it were a sunny day? ("Chain" the responses.)

JOURNAL WRITING: Students Write

Sy Write about the things you do on rainy or lonely days.

CHAPTER 5—Charlotte; CHAPTER 6—Summer Days

VOCABULARY:

C

address (speak)	deny	gratified	lair	stirring
anxious	desperately	hoist	nearsighted	tangled
appropriate	errand	inheritance	objectionable	unremitting
blunder	gleam	jubilee	salutations	untenable

PREREADING DISCUSSION: Teacher Writes On Board

An What are some things you like and dislike about spiders? (List the responses.)

POSTREADING: Teacher Reads; Discussion; Teacher Writes On Board

Read aloud the passage beginning, "When the first gosling poked its gray-green head through the goose's feathers," and ending with, "May I offer my sincere congratulations!"

Ev What can you tell about Charlotte by the way she talks? (List the responses.)

JOURNAL WRITING: Students Write

Sy Write how you feel about Charlotte from the goose's point of view.

CHAPTER 7—Bad News; CHAPTER 8—A Talk At Home

VOCABULARY:

C

anesthetic	campaign	envy	rambled
briskly	conspiracy	hysterics	rigid
butchered	conversation	imagination	vaguely

PREREADING DISCUSSION:

An What kinds of things do you consider to be "bad news"?

Ev How do you react to bad news?

POSTREADING DISCUSSION:

Ev Do you think Mrs. Arable should be concerned about Fern? Why or why not?

Ev What would Fern have to do for you to be concerned about her?

JOURNAL WRITING: Students Write

Sy Write a note to Dr. Dorian from Mrs. Arable about her concern for Fern.

CHAPTER 9—Wilbur's Boast; CHAPTER 10—An Explosion

VOCABULARY:

C

affectionately	discouraged	hastily	resist	summon
astride	drowsed	hayloft	sedentary	troupe
curiosity	embarrassment	neglect	spinnerets	
delicate	gullible	occasional	straddled	

PREREADING DISCUSSION: Teacher Writes On Board

An If you wanted to spin a web, how would you do it? (List the responses.)

POSTREADING DISCUSSION: Teacher Writes On Board

Ev What do you think would have happened if Avery had captured Charlotte?

JOURNAL WRITING: Teacher Reads; Students Write

Read aloud the section beginning, "Twilight settled over Zuckerman's barn," and ending with, "The thought of death came to him and he began to tremble with fear."

Sy Write a beautiful description of a summer's evening spent in your area. In the midst of your writing, break the mood by recalling something sad or troubling.

CHARLOTTE'S WEB

CHAPTER 11—The Miracle; CHAPTER 12—A Meeting

VOCABULARY:

C

assembled	exertions	idiosyncrasy	sensational	uttered
bewilderment	glistened	miraculous	solemnly	wondrous

PREREADING DISCUSSION: Teacher Writes On Board

An List adjectives in your journal that describe something wonderful or great.

POSTREADING DISCUSSION: Teacher Writes On Board

C Skim chapters 11 and 12 to find adjectives describing something wonderful.

JOURNAL WRITING: Students Write

Sy Choose a word for Charlotte's web. Write a conversation to convince the animals to accept the word. Make sure each animal stays "true to character."

CHAPTER 13—Good Progress; CHAPTER 14—Dr. Dorian

VOCABULARY:

C

admiration	astonishing	merciless	radial	rummaging
aeronaut	fascinating	orb	radiant	sociable
associate	fidget	predict	remarkable	thrashing

PREREADING DISCUSSION:

Ev How do you think Charlotte is going to save Wilbur with words?

Ev What other problems can be solved using only words?

POSTREADING DISCUSSION: Students Skim Chapter; Teacher Writes On Board

Ev Do you agree with Dr. Dorian's advice? Why or why not?

An How was Dr. Dorian's advice similar to Mr. Arable's advice in chapter 8?

Ev Why do you think Mrs. Arable listened more to the doctor than to her husband?

JOURNAL WRITING: Teacher Reads; Students Write

Read aloud the lullaby that Charlotte sings to Wilbur. (Listen to the images Charlotte uses that are special to Wilbur.)

Sy Write your own lullaby for Wilbur and include one of his favorite things.

CHAPTER 15—The Crickets; CHAPTER 16—Off to the Fair

VOCABULARY:

C

confident	inconvenient	monotonous	scampered	trampled
distinguish	interrupted	pummel	smudge	trickling
heave	lacerated	sac	surpass	tussle

PREREADING DISCUSSION:

Ev   Do you think all of this attention will go to Wilbur's head? Why?

POSTREADING DISCUSSION:

Ap   Explain how Wilbur's life is literally hanging by a thread.

Ev   How do you think Charlotte is feeling about this responsibility?

Ev   Is she better able to deal with the thought of death because she has to kill to survive? Why or why not?

JOURNAL WRITING:

Sy   Write about what you would do and see at the fair from Templeton's viewpoint.

CHAPTER 17—Uncle; CHAPTER 18—The Cool of the Evening

VOCABULARY:

C

ascended	detected	enormous	moistened	personality

PREREADING DISCUSSION: Teacher Writes On Board

An   What kinds of things can people and animals do at the fair? (List the responses.)

POSTREADING DISCUSSION: Teacher Writes On Board

Ev   What do you think Charlotte is making and why?

JOURNAL WRITING: Students Write

Sy   Explain "your day at the fair" from Fern's point of view.

CHARLOTTE'S WEB

CHAPTER 19—The Egg Sac; CHAPTER 20—The Horn of Triumph

VOCABULARY:

C

acute	distinguished	languish	suspiciously	unconscious
admiring	hoarse	revive	triumph	unique

PREREADING DISCUSSION:

Ev What changes do you think the egg sac will bring to the story?

POSTREADING DISCUSSION: Teacher Writes On Board

Ev How would your reaction to the prize be different from Wilbur's reaction?

JOURNAL WRITING: Students Write

Sy Write about what you would do and see at the fair from Templeton's viewpoint.

CHAPTER 21—Last Day; CHAPTER 22—A Warm Wind

VOCABULARY:

C

abuse	assured	drearily	gorge	strain
accompany	daintily	gigantic	solemn	tranquil

PREREADING DISCUSSION:

Ev How would you say good-bye to a good friend? Find out how Wilbur handles it.

POSTREADING DISCUSSION: Teacher Reads; Discussion; Teacher Writes On Board

Read aloud the passage beginning, "She never moved again," and ending with, "No one was with her when she died."

An How was Charlotte's death like the disassembly of the fair? (List the responses.)

JOURNAL WRITING: Students Draw And Write

Design a tombstone for Charlotte. Write a meaningful description of Charlotte from Wilbur's point of view that expresses what a great friend she was.

CULMINATING ACTIVITIES

POSTREADING DISCUSSION:

Ev Who was your favorite/least favorite character? Why?

Ev What was your favorite/least favorite part of the book? Why?

JOURNAL WRITING: Students Write

Ev Have each student choose one of the following culminating activities.
• Write about Wilbur's triumph at the fair.
• Write about how Charlotte wanted to say good-bye to Wilbur.

CHARLOTTE'S WEB

MATH

COMPARATIVE SIZES:

Instruct the students to cut out life-size silhouettes of the animals mentioned in the story (pig, rat, spider, sheep, goose, etc.). Have the students work individually or in small groups to compare the sizes of the animals (length, width, weight, etc.). (Examples: A pig is three times as tall as a goose. A sheep is twenty times taller than a rat.) Graph the results.

SOCIAL STUDIES

COLLECTION:

Have the students compile collections of all the things Templeton might have collected. Ask each student to discuss the similarities and differences between Templeton's collection and his or her collection.

DEATH/DYING:

Discuss as a group ways that people deal with death and dying and the way Wilbur dealt with it. (Read Leo Buscaglia's *The Fall Of Freddie The Leaf*, Charles B. Flack , Inc., 1982.)

SCIENCE

SPIDERS:

Have the students study the life cycle of the spider.

PIGS/RATS:

Have the students compare the life cycles of pigs and rats.

FINE ARTS

SEWING:

Have the students make spider webs using white thread or yarn and black construction paper. Instruct each student to stitch in the web a word describing Wilbur.

MODEL:

Instruct the students to construct a model of the crate that was made to transport Wilbur to the fair. Place a paper-mache replica of Wilbur in the crate and a replica of Charlotte's web in the corner.

JAMES AND THE GIANT PEACH

CHAPTER 1

Ap 1. On another piece of paper, tell what would you have packed and explain why.

K 2. List the kinds of punishment James was promised on another piece of paper.

An 3. On another piece of paper, tell what happened in this chapter.

CHAPTER 2

Ap 4. Recite the poem *Aunt Sponge and Aunt Spike* with a friend.

An 5. On another piece of paper, list other things children might be doing that James would want to do.

Ev 6. What would you do if you were James and your aunts threatened you? _____

_____

An 7. On another piece of paper, tell what happened in this chapter.

CHAPTER 3

Ev 8. Who do you think the little old man was and why did he want to help James?

_____

C 9. On another piece of paper, draw and label the ingredients that made the magic green things.

An 10. On another piece of paper, tell what happened in this chapter.

CHAPTER 4

Ev 11. On another piece of paper, tell what would happen if an insect got some of the magic.

An 12. On another piece of paper, tell what happened in this chapter.

© 1990 by Incentive Publications, Inc., Nashville, TN.

JAMES AND THE GIANT PEACH   Individual Learning Unit Cont.

CHAPTER 5

Ap   **13.** If you were James, how would you have handled the magic green things?

_____

Ev   **14.** What do you think will get the full power of the magic? Why? _____

_____

An   **15.** On another piece of paper, tell what happened in this chapter.

CHAPTER 6

Ev   **16.** What do you think would have happened if the aunts had eaten the peach?

_____

Ev   **17.** What title would you give this chapter and why? _____

_____

An   **18.** On another piece of paper, tell what happened in this chapter.

CHAPTER 7

C   **19.** On another piece of paper, list words or phrases in this chapter meaning "big."

Ev   **20.** On another piece of paper, list two ways Aunt Spiker can make money with a large peach.

An   **21.** On another piece of paper, tell what happened in this chapter.

CHAPTER 8

C   **22.** Make a sign that gives the costs for adults and children to see the peaches.

Sy   **23.** On another piece of paper, write a newspaper article about the peach.

Ap   **24.** On another piece of paper tell what you'd do if your aunts treated you like James' aunts treated him.

An   **25.** On another piece of paper, tell what happened in this chapter.

CHAPTER 9

Sy **26.** On another piece of paper, explain why James is afraid of the dark.

Ap **27.** On another piece of paper, tell how and when the hole was made in the peach.

An **28.** On another piece of paper, tell what happened in this chapter.

CHAPTER 10

C **29.** What is another name for a peach stone? _____

Ev **30.** How do you think the creatures that welcomed James knew he was coming?

_____

Ev **31.** What title would you give this chapter and why?_____

_____

An **32.** On another piece of paper, tell what happened in this chapter.

CHAPTER 11

K **33.** On another piece of paper, tell what creatures James saw in the peach.

C **34.** On another piece of paper, explain what the Ladybug meant when she said, "You are one of us now, didn't you know that? You are one of the crew."

An **35.** On another piece of paper, tell what happened in this chapter.

CHAPTER 12

C **36.** Describe Centipede, Earthworm, and Grasshopper on another piece of paper.

An **37.** On another piece of paper, list ways that being with the creatures were different from living with James' aunts.

Ev **38.** On another piece of paper, tell how you feel about the Centipede.

An **39.** On another piece of paper, tell what happened in this chapter.

JAMES AND THE GIANT PEACH Individual Learning Unit Cont.

CHAPTER 13

Ap **40.** Tie a knot in two sets of shoelaces. See how long it takes you to undo the knots. Then calculate how long it would take to untie twenty-one pairs of shoes?

Ev **41.** What title would you give this chapter and why? _____
_____

An **42.** On another piece of paper, tell what happened in this chapter.

CHAPTER 14

Ev **43.** On another piece of paper, tell how you think the Ladybug knew that James' aunts were repulsive.

Ev **44.** What title would you give this chapter and why? _____
_____

An **45.** On another piece of paper, tell what happened in this chapter.

CHAPTER 15

Ev **46.** What do you think the aunts would have done to James had they known where he was? Why? _____
_____

Ev **47.** What title would you give this chapter and why? _____
_____

An **48.** On another piece of paper, tell what happened in this chapter.

CHAPTER 16

Ev **49.** On another piece of paper, tell how the chocolate factory owners probably felt.

Ap **50.** On another piece of paper, tell what you'd do if you saw the peach rolling toward you.

JAMES AND THE GIANT PEACH Individual Learning Unit Cont.

CHAPTER 17

Ap **51.** If you were inside the peach, where would you think the peach had landed? Why? _____

_____

Ev **52.** What title would you give this chapter and why? _____

_____

An **53.** On another piece of paper, tell what happened in this chapter.

CHAPTER 18

An **54.** On another piece of paper, tell how you are alike and different from James.

C **55.** On another piece of paper, draw and label three things the Centipede said he had eaten.

K **56.** On another piece of paper, tell how James helped the others in this chapter.

An **57.** On another piece of paper, tell what happened in this chapter.

CHAPTER 19

C **58.** On another piece of paper, explain what this means: "Panic and pandemonium broke out immediately on top of the peach."

Ev **59.** What title would you give this chapter and why? _____

_____

An **60.** On another piece of paper, tell what happened in this chapter.

CHAPTER 20

C **61.** On another piece of paper, tell how the Earthworm reacted to James' plan.

Ev **62.** On another piece of paper, tell whether or not you think James' plan will work and explain why.

An **63.** On another piece of paper, tell what happened in this chapter.

CHAPTER 21

C   **64.** On another piece of paper, explain what this statement about James means: "He was the captain now, and everyone knew it."

Ap   **65.** On another piece of paper, tell how Earthworm, Centipede, Grasshopper, Spider, Silkworm, Glowworm, and Ladybug felt about the plan.

An   **66.** On another piece of paper, tell what happened in this chapter.

CHAPTER 22

C   **67.** On another sheet of paper, draw each character carrying out his or her "job."

Ev   **68.** What title would you give this chapter and why? _____
_____

An   **69.** On another piece of paper, tell what happened in this chapter.

CHAPTER 23

Ev   **70.** On another piece of paper, tell what you would do if you were on the ship and the captain reported all of those strange sights.

Ev   **71.** What title would you give this chapter and why?_____
_____

An   **72.** On another piece of paper, tell what happened in this chapter.

CHAPTER 24

An   **73.** On another piece of paper, explain how "short horned" and "long horned" grasshoppers are alike and different.

Ev   **74.** How do you feel about the Centipede's remark about James' ears? Why? __
_____

Ev   **75.** What title would you give this chapter and why? _____
_____

An   **76.** On another piece of paper, tell what happened in this chapter.

JAMES AND THE GIANT PEACH Individual Learning Unit Cont.

CHAPTER 25

C **77.** On another piece of paper, describe the services that each of these characters performs: Earthworm, Ladybug, Centipede, Spider.

Sy **78.** On another piece of paper, write a limerick about a character from the story.

An **79.** On another piece of paper, tell what happened in this chapter.

CHAPTER 26

An **80.** How is James different now from what he was in the beginning of the story?__
_____

Ev **81.** What title would you give this chapter and why?_____
_____

An **82.** On another piece of paper, tell what happened in this chapter.

CHAPTER 27

An **83.** On another piece of paper, describe how traveling on the peach is similar to and different from traveling on an airplane.

Ev **84.** How would things have been different if Centipede had not been on the trip? _____
_____

An **85.** On another piece of paper, tell what happened in this chapter.

CHAPTER 28

Ev **86.** Do you think the Centipede will understand the Earthworm better after this experience? Why or why not?_____
_____

An **87.** On another piece of paper, tell what happened in this chapter.

© 1990 by Incentive Publications, Inc., Nashville, TN.

JAMES AND THE GIANT PEACH Individual Learning Unit Cont.

CHAPTER 29

Ap 88. Why do you think rainbow paint dries very quickly and very hard? _____
_____

Ev 89. On another piece of paper, tell whose plan for helping Centipede you like best. Why? _____
_____

An 90. On another piece of paper, tell what happened in this chapter.

CHAPTER 30

Sy 91. On another piece of paper, write a limerick from the Earthworm's point of view (five lines of 8, 8, 5, 5, 8 syllables respectively).

Ap 92. What do you think would have happened if the water had not come out of the sky? _____
_____

An 93. On another piece of paper, tell what happened in this chapter.

CHAPTER 31

Ev 94. On another piece of paper, explain why you agree or disagree that all of the work the cloudmen do is "sinister magic."

Ev 95. What title would you give this chapter and why? _____
_____

An 96. On another piece of paper, tell what happened in this chapter.

CHAPTER 32

An 97. On another piece of paper, tell how America was different from England.

Ev 98. What title would you give this chapter and why? _____
_____

An 99. On another piece of paper, tell what happened in this chapter.

© 1990 by Incentive Publications, Inc., Nashville, TN.

JAMES AND THE GIANT PEACH Individual Learning Unit Cont.

CHAPTER 33

Ap **100.** Why do you think the people in New York thought the peach was a giant bomb?

Sy **101.** On another piece of paper, write what you think the mayor of New York said to the president of the United States? (Remember to use quotation marks.)

Ev **102.** What title would you give this chapter and why? _____
_____

An **103.** On another piece of paper, tell what happened in this chapter.

CHAPTER 34

Sy **104.** On another piece of paper, write what you think the pilot radioed to the control tower when he came upon the peach. (Don't forget to use quotation marks.)

An **105.** On another piece of paper, tell what happened in this chapter.

CHAPTER 35

K **106.** On another piece of paper, list the ways people reacted to the falling peach.

Ev **107.** What title would you give this chapter and why? _____
_____

An **108.** On another piece of paper, tell what happened in this chapter.

CHAPTER 36

Ev **109.** What would have happened if James and everyone on the peach had not held on to the stem?

Ev **110.** What title would you give this chapter and why? _____
_____

An **111.** On another piece of paper, tell what happened in this chapter.

CHAPTER 37

Ev | **112.** On another piece of paper, tell what you think would have happened to the creatures on the peach if James had not been there to introduce them.

Ap | **113.** On another piece of paper, tell how you would have reacted to the peculiar sight of the creatures on the peach if you were a police officer or fire fighter.

An | **114.** On another piece of paper, tell what happened in this chapter.

CHAPTER 38

An | **115.** On another piece of paper, describe how James and his friends on the peach were first viewed as a threat and then as heroes.

C | **116.** On another piece of paper, draw and label the people and vehicles in the parade.

C | **117.** On another piece of paper, explain what this means: "...to some people it looked as though the Pied Piper of Hamlin had suddenly descended upon New York."

CHAPTER 39

Ev | **118.** What title would you give this chapter and why? _____

_____

An | **119.** On another piece of paper, tell what happened in this chapter.

JAMES AND THE GIANT PEACH

1. Make up a play or puppet show to tell what would have happened to James if he had not dropped the bag of magic things.

2. Construct a model of one of the following things and be prepared to explain it:

- the cloudmen city

- what the cloudmen used to make different kinds of weather

- the inside of the peach and everyone in it

- the peach on the Empire State Building

3. Write a "captain's log" describing all of the adventures that happened on the peach. (Tape-record the log if you wish.)

4. Dress up like one of the characters and tell about your experiences.

5. Write a poem or song about the adventures James encountered on the peach. Perform the song or record it.

6. Tape-record some of the songs and poems in the book. Between each song and poem, record a brief explanation of the events related through the song or poem.

7. Design a colorful travel brochure advertising a trip on the giant peach. Make the brochure so appealing that others will want to ride on the peach.

JAMES AND THE GIANT PEACH

PRELIMINARY ACTIVITIES

GETTING READY TO READ:

K | Who are the author and illustrator? *Roald Dahl; Nancy Ekholm Burkert*

Ap | Where do you think the story takes place? *answers will vary*

PREREADING DISCUSSION: Teacher Writes On Board

An | How is a peach useful? What kinds of animals/insects live in or around peaches?

JOURNAL WRITING: Discussion; Students Write

Ev | How would the insects named in the prereading discussion get along together?

CHAPTERS 1 - 3

VOCABULARY:

C |

beckon	enormous	ghastly	nuisance	ramshackle
desolate	extraordinary	hideous	overwhelm	spectacles
disgusting	fantastic	luminous	peculiar	wistful

PREREADING DISCUSSION:

Ev | What are the most terrible things you could imagine happening in your life?

POSTREADING DISCUSSION:

Ev | If you were James, how would you deal with your loneliness?

JOURNAL WRITING: Discussion; Students Write

Ev | How would you use the magic green things if you were James?

CHAPTERS 4 - 6

VOCABULARY:

C |

blossom	froth	marvelous	pulp	swerve
burrow	furious	precious	scrabbling	vanish

PREREADING DISCUSSION:

Ap | How would you keep the green things safe?

JAMES AND THE GIANT PEACH

POSTREADING DISCUSSION:

| Ev | What do you think would happen if the aunts ate the peach?

JOURNAL WRITING: Students Write

| Sy | If you had tasted the brew, how would you use your powers?

CHAPTERS 7 - 9

VOCABULARY:

| C |

| absolutely | inspect | miraculous | seething | wander |
| cautiously | massive | murmur | tremendous | |

PREREADING DISCUSSION:

| An | What descriptive words can you think of to describe "bigness"?

POSTREADING DISCUSSION:

| Ap | Have you ever had a great feeling of excitement? What did it feel like?

JOURNAL WRITING: Students Write

Describe a time you knew something exciting was going to happen and it did.

CHAPTERS 10 - 12

VOCABULARY:

| C |

| colossal | famished | interrupt | primly | shriek |
| disagreeable | hysterics | murky | recline | wither |

PREREADING DISCUSSION: Teacher Writes On Board

| Ev | If you were James, what would you do about the hole in the peach?

POSTREADING DISCUSSION: Teacher Writes On Board

| An | How are the creatures James meets frightening and friendly?

JOURNAL WRITING: Students Write

| Ev | What would have happened if James had not gone into the hole?

JAMES AND THE GIANT PEACH

CHAPTERS 13 - 15

VOCABULARY:

ambled	dilemma	hammock	jostle	panicked
complicated	gossamer	heave	literal	repulsive
desolate	gracious	insidious	obvious	venomous

PREREADING DISCUSSION:

 If you were James, where would you want to go?

POSTREADING DISCUSSION:

 How do you feel about what happened to James' aunts? Why?

JOURNAL WRITING: Teacher Reads; Students Write

Read the Centipede's poem in chapter 14.

 Write a poem about creatures you might meet if you were with James.

CHAPTERS 16 - 18

VOCABULARY:

affectionately	giddy	hurtle	perish	starvation
chaos	greedy	indescribable	scrumptious	trifle
disentangle	grisly	paddock	stampede	vertically

PREREADING DISCUSSION:

Ev What do you think will happen when the peach rolls down the hill?

POSTREADING DISCUSSION:

Ap What kinds of adventures can James and his friends have on the sea?

JOURNAL WRITING: Students Chant; Students Write

Read the Centipede's song in chapter 18.

Sy Write a song about how a peach would compare to three of your favorite foods.

JAMES AND THE GIANT PEACH

CHAPTERS 19 - 21

VOCABULARY:

C
aghast	froth	pathetic	perambulator	threshing
coax	martyr	pandemonium	scuttled	

PREREADING DISCUSSION:

Ap What kinds of problems might James and his friends encounter at sea?

POSTREADING DISCUSSION:

Ev How would things be different if the spider and silkworm weren't there?

JOURNAL WRITING: Students Write

Sy Write about what the situation is and what James plans to do about it.

CHAPTERS 22 - 24

VOCABULARY:

C
apologize	clambered	majestically	rambunctious	telescope
ascent	exhorting	precisely	teeming	tethered

PREREADING DISCUSSION: Teacher Writes On Board

An What are the advantages in working in a group versus working alone?

POSTREADING DISCUSSION:

Ap In what other ways would you have celebrated with the group?

JOURNAL WRITING: Teacher Reads; Students Write

Read the passage in chapter 24 beginning, "'My dear young fellow,' the Old-Green-Grasshopper said gently, 'there are a whole lot of things in this world of ours that you haven't started wondering about yet,'" and ending, "'You ought to take a peek in the mirror some day and see for yourself.'"

Sy Where else could you have ears? How would these changes affect your life?

JAMES AND THE GIANT PEACH

CHAPTERS 25 - 27

VOCABULARY:

C

argument	infuriated	loathsome	obvious	teeter
essential	insulting	menacing	quiver	trifle
imbeciles	launched	modest	stealthy	vital

PREREADING DISCUSSION: Teacher Writes On Board

An What services do you think each of the insects provides in the garden?

POSTREADING DISCUSSION:

Sy What do you like and dislike about the Centipede?

JOURNAL WRITING: Students Write

Make up a story about how the cloudmen make rain.

CHAPTERS 28 -30

VOCABULARY:

C

deluge	enthralled	groped	monstrous	somersaults
dodging	faucet	hypnotized	pelting	swarming
encased	flabbergasted	malevolent	shimmering	wretched

PREREADING DISCUSSION:

Ap Think of some make-believe ways that rainbows could be made.

POSTREADING DISCUSSION:

Ev What might have happened if the Centipede had remained in the paint?

JOURNAL WRITING: Students Write

Sy Write an article from the cloudmen's point of view about the incident with the peach and the rainbow.

JAMES AND THE GIANT PEACH

CHAPTERS 31 - 33

VOCABULARY:

C

blizzard	funnel	melancholy	sinister	summon
cramped	hovering	pavement	sirens	toboggan
frisking	immense	smithereens	soot	vast

PREREADING DISCUSSION:

Ev What other kinds of activities do you think cloudmen do? How are they helpful or harmful?

POSTREADING DISCUSSION:

Ev How can James let the people know that he and his friends are not a threat?

JOURNAL WRITING: Students Write

Sy Write a radio and television announcement the people of the United States might have heard about the peach. Be prepared to read the announcements.

CHAPTERS 34 - 36

VOCABULARY:

C

dangling	flung	plummet	squelch	taper
desperate	pinnacle	shelter	stupor	

PREREADING DISCUSSION:

Ev What would you do if you thought you were going to die?

POSTREADING DISCUSSION: Teacher Writes On Board

An List adjectives to describe the feelings of those on the peach and those in New York. How are they similar?

JOURNAL WRITING: Students Write

Sy What should James say to introduce himself and the others on the peach to those in New York so that the people will not be afraid?

JAMES AND THE GIANT PEACH

CHAPTERS 37 -39

VOCABULARY:

| C |

binoculars   eccentricity   gigantic   marvel   procession
chaperone   entrancing   Gorgon   monstrous   ticker tape
commotion   gape   limousine   monument

PREREADING DISCUSSION:

Ev If you were a New Yorker and knew the thing in the sky wasn't a bomb, what else might you think it could be?

POSTREADING DISCUSSION:

An How is James different from the way he was before the peach appeared?

JOURNAL WRITING: Teacher & Students Read; Students Write

Read James' poem in chapter 37.

Ap Write a poem to introduce each character just as James did.

CULMINATING ACTIVITIES

POSTREADING DISCUSSION:

Ev Do you think James and his friends ever get homesick for England? Explain.

STORY FRAME: Discussion; Students Read; Teacher Writes On Board; Students Fill In Story Frames

C Have the students fill in the characters and setting on their story frames. Discuss the plot and then have the students review their chapter summaries. Ask the class to brainstorm major events in the story (list on board). Consolidate statements and ideas and then have the students fill in the summary sections of their story frames.

JOURNAL WRITING: Students Write

Ev Ask each student to choose one of the following culminating activities:

- What other jobs might each of James' friends have had? Explain the jobs.
- How would the story be different if James hadn't climbed into the peach hole?
- Write a newspaper story about the giant peach.

JAMES AND THE GIANT PEACH

MATH

GRAPHING:

Have each student graph twenty-one pairs (or more) of shoes (like Centipede wore) according to size, color, type, material, where made and bought, etc.

MEASURING:

Cook with peaches. Make pies, tarts, or cobblers. Have the students increase the recipe to feed the class, measure the amounts, and help to prepare the food.

DRAW TO SCALE:

Ask each student to draw the skylines of New York and his or her hometown "to scale." Students will have fun comparing the skylines!

SOCIAL STUDIES

MAPPING:

Instruct the students to draw maps of England, the Atlantic Ocean, and the United States. Then have the students plot the course of the peach from England to New York and label each adventure "along the way."

NEW YORK:

Lead the students in a study of New York City and ask them to compare New York to their hometown.

SCIENCE

EXPERIMENT:

Have the students subject a peach to all of the experiences in the book and record the results over a period of days (place it on the ground, float it in water, poke holes in it, skewer it on a sharp object, deluge it with water, etc.).

WEATHER:

Have the students study what "makes" clouds, rainbows, rain, hail, etc. Contrast the findings with what the cloudmen do.

FINE ARTS

DIORAMA:

Ask each student to make a diorama illustrating an event in the story.

Sarah, Plain And Tall

SARAH, PLAIN AND TALL

CHAPTER 1

Rewrite sentences 1 - 3 on another piece of paper. Look up the underlined words in the dictionary.

`C`   **1.** It was <u>dusk</u>.

`C`   **2.** He was <u>homely</u>.

`C`   **3.** Do you have <u>opinions</u> about cats?

`K`   **4.** Who were Lotti and Nick? _____

_____

`Ap`   **5.** On another piece of paper, tell why Caleb had questions about his mother.

`Sy`   **6.** If you didn't know one of your parents, what questions would you ask about him or her? List them on another piece of paper.

`K`   **7.** What did Mama sing about? _____

_____

`K`   **8.** Why doesn't Papa sing anymore? _____

_____

`Ev`   **9.** On another piece of paper, tell how you'd feel if you were one of the children.

`Ap`   **10.** What title would you give this chapter and why? _____

_____

CHAPTER 2

Rewrite sentences 11 - 13 on another piece of paper. Look up the underlined words in the dictionary.

`C`   **11.** I <u>prefer</u> to build bookshelves and paint.

`C`   **12.** I am <u>enclosing</u> a book of seabirds.

`C`   **13.** You are loud and <u>pesky</u>.

`An`   **14.** Judging from the letters the children received, what questions do you think each one asked? Write them on another piece of paper.

`C`   **15.** How did Anna and Caleb feel about Sarah's visit? _____

_____

K **16.** What happened during the time after Papa mailed his letter and before he received Sarah's letter?

An **17.** What does Sarah mean when she says she is "plain and tall"? _____

_____

K **18.** Why was Caleb excited about what was written at the bottom of the letter?

_____

Ap **19.** What title would you give this chapter and why?

CHAPTER 3

Rewrite sentences 20 - 22 on another piece of paper. Look up the underlined words in the dictionary.

C **20.** Papa drove off along the dirt road to <u>fetch</u> Sarah.

C **21.** The wagon <u>clattered</u> into the yard.

C **22.** Blue <u>flax</u> dried in a vase on the night table.

K **23.** On another piece of paper, list the chores Anna and Caleb did.

An **24.** How old do you think Caleb is? What did he do in this chapter to make you think so? _____

_____

Ap **25.** How did the children feel about the visit?_____

_____

C/Ap **26.** What did Sarah mean when she said, "I wished everything was as perfect as the stone"? _____

_____

Ap **27.** What title would you give this chapter and why?_____

_____

CHAPTER 4

Rewrite sentences 28 - 30 on another piece of paper. Look up the underlined words in the dictionary.

C   **28.** "A <u>scallop</u>," she told us, picking up the shells.

C   **29.** Wild roses climbed up the <u>paddock</u> fence.

C   **30.** We sat on the porch and heard the <u>rustle</u> of cows in the grasses.

K   **31.** How did Papa and Anna act with Sarah? How did Caleb act with Sarah? ___
_____

C   **32.** What does this mean: "Papa sang as if he had never stopped singing"? ____
_____

Ap   **33.** What title would you give this chapter and why? _____
_____

C   **34.** Read this summary and fill in the blanks with the correct word(s).

Sarah showed the children her _____ collection. She

picked _____ , cut _____ , and then sang

with the family. The song was about _____ .

CHAPTER 5

Rewrite sentences 35 - 37 on another piece of paper. Look up the underlined words in the dictionary.

C   **35.** Sarah sank her fingers into the <u>coarse</u> wool.

C   **36.** Bill and I found a sand <u>dune</u> all our own.

C   **37.** Next to the barn was Papa's <u>mound</u> of hay.

C   **38.** How did Sarah feel when she found the dead lamb? What did she do that let you know how she felt? _____
_____

Ap   **39.** Caleb, Anna, and Sarah talked about the first word they ever said. What was your first word? Why do you think you said that word first? _____
_____

An 40. How is the dune picture the same as and different from your picture? _____

_____

K 41. Out of what material did Papa make the dune for Sarah? _____

_____

Ap 42. On another piece of paper, list other things you could use to make a dune.

K 43. Which one of Sarah's drawings had "something missing"? _____

_____

Ev 44. How would this chapter be different if Papa hadn't made the dune? _____

_____

C 45. Read this summary and fill in the blanks with the correct word(s).

Sarah touched _____ for the first time and she drew

_____ to send to her _____ in

Maine. When she talked about sand _____ , Papa made

one out of _____ .

CHAPTER 6

Rewrite sentences 46 - 48 on another piece of paper. Look up the underlined words in the dictionary.

C 46. When the <u>chores</u> were done, we sat in the meadow.

C 47. Sarah and I watched him jump over <u>gullies</u>.

C 48. Sarah <u>treaded</u> water.

K 49. What had Papa taught Sarah to do? _____

_____

An 50. On another piece of paper, list things that happen on the prairie in winter.

K 51. What did Papa do to keep the children from getting lost in storms? _____

_____

K 52. After swimming, Anna said she slept and "dreamed a perfect dream." Write about her perfect dream on another piece of paper.

Ap 53. What title would you give this chapter and why? _____

_____

C 54. Read this summary and fill in the blanks with the correct word(s).

Papa taught Sarah how to _____ the fields. When Sarah

was done, she asked the children about what _____ was like.

When it got _____ , Sarah jumped into the _____ to

swim. She taught Caleb and Anna how to _____ .

CHAPTER 7

Rewrite sentences 55 - 57. Look up the underlined words in the dictionary.

C 55. The chickens followed, scratching <u>primly</u> in the dirt.

C 56. Maggie helped <u>hitch</u> the horses to the plow.

C 57. There are three old aunts who <u>squawk</u> like crows.

K 58. What did the neighbors come to do? _____

Ap 59. On another piece of paper, list girls' names that also are names of flowers.

Sy 60. On another piece of paper, design a colorful quilt.

K 61. Where did Maggie live previously? _____

C 62. On another piece of paper, explain what Maggie meant when she said, "There are always things to miss no matter where you are."

An 63. On another piece of paper, compare Maggie and Sarah.

C 64. Read this summary and fill in the blanks with the correct word(s).

The neighbors came to _____ . Maggie brought Sarah

some _____ . The women talked about being

_____ . Sarah learned that to get around on the prairie she

would have to learn to _____ . When the men came in

from the fields, everyone _____ . When the neighbors

had gone, Papa brought Sarah _____ .

SARAH, PLAIN AND TALL — Individual Learning Unit Cont.

CHAPTER 8

Rewrite sentences 65 - 67 on another piece of paper. Look up the underlined words in the dictionary.

C 65. "This woman does," said Sarah <u>crisply</u>.

C 66. "I shook my head, <u>weary</u> with Caleb's questions.

C 67. There was a hiss of wind, a sudden <u>pungent</u> smell.

C 68. How did Sarah feel at the first part of this chapter? What in the story makes you aware of how Sarah feels? _____

_____

Ev 69. On another piece of paper, explain what Caleb meant when he said, "Look what is missing from your drawing."

C 70. When Papa put his arm around Sarah, Caleb "...smiled and smiled until he could smile no more." Why? _____

_____

Ap 71. What title would you give this chapter and why? _____

_____

C 72. Read this summary and fill in the blanks with the correct word(s).

In the morning, Sarah had _____ with Papa. He didn't want

her to _____ . But a _____

was coming and she and Papa worked _____

together instead. When the storm came, the family gathered the animals

together and _____ until morning.

CHAPTER 9

Rewrite sentences 73 - 75 on another piece of paper. Look up the underlined words in the dictionary.

C 73. Seal leaped on the fence to <u>groom</u> herself.

C 74. Sarah's chickens <u>scuttled</u> along behind me.

C 75. Caleb <u>nudged</u> me.

K   **76.** What was Papa's promise to Sarah? _____

_____

C   **77.** Why did Caleb and Anna cry? _____

_____

An   **78.** On another piece of paper, list reasons why Sarah might want to leave or stay.

Ev   **79.** How would you have felt if you had seen Sarah coming back on the wagon?

_____

C   **80.** How had Sarah "brought the sea"? _____

_____

Ap   **81.** What title would you give this chapter and why? _____

_____

C   **82.** Read this summary and fill in the blanks with the correct phrases.

After the _____ , Papa and Sarah _____

the damaged field. Papa also taught her to _____ .

Sarah drove the _____ alone. Caleb

was worried because he _____ . In the evening,

Sarah returned. She gave us a present. It was _____ .

Caleb said happily, "Sarah has brought _____ !" Soon

Papa and Sarah would be _____ .

AFTER READING

An   **83.** On another piece of paper, describe Caleb, Anna, Papa, and Sarah.

Ap   **84.** Which character is most like you? Why? _____

_____

Ev   **85.** What part of the book did you like best? What part did you like least?_____

_____

SARAH, PLAIN AND TALL

1. Prepare a shell collection. Be prepared to tell about each shell.

2. Design and sew your own quilt.

3. Make a scrapbook for one of the characters. Share it with the class.

4. Draw and explain pictures Sarah would have sent to William.

5. Create one collage using prairie pictures and colors and another collage using seashore pictures and colors. Display the collages in the classroom.

6. Dress and act like one of the characters. Tell the class what happened to you in the book.

7. Cook stew and biscuits for your reading group or for the entire class. Share the recipes! Or, pack a lunch of homemade bread, cheese, and lemonade for everyone to share.

8. Map Sarah's trip from Maine to a prairie state (you decide which one). Or, make a map of the farm and label *everything*.

9. Compile a book of songs the family might have sung. Share it with the class.

10. Plant or draw a colorful garden consisting of the plants Sarah had in the story. Label each plant.

SARAH, PLAIN AND TALL

PRELIMINARY ACTIVITIES

GETTING READY TO READ:

K | Who is the author? *Patricia MacLachlan*

K | Has the book won any awards? *Newbery Medal for most distinguished contribution to American literature for children*

Ap | Where do you think the story takes place? *answers will vary*

K | What do you think the story is about? *answers will vary*

PREREADING DISCUSSION: Teacher Writes On Board

An | What is the difference between a prairie farm and a seashore? (List the responses.)

JOURNAL WRITING: Students Write

Ap | How would you feel if you had to move from the seashore to the prairie farm or vice versa? (Have the students list adjectives in their journals.)

An | Discuss what might make students want to stay in or leave their homes. Have the students list phrases in their journals under the headings "Stay" and "Leave."

CHAPTER 1

VOCABULARY:

C |

crackled	harshly	hollow	murmured	shuffling
dusk	hearthstone	homely	plain	stirred
feisty	holler	horrid	prairie	wretched

PREREADING DISCUSSION: Teacher Writes On Board

Ev | How do you feel when you sing?

An | Discuss times when you want to sing and when you don't want to sing. (List the responses).

POSTREADING DISCUSSION: Teacher Writes On Board

C | Tell how these characters feel about singing: Papa, Caleb, Anna. (Circle responses from prereading lists that students can substantiate in the chapter.)

An | How are their feelings similar to and different from how you feel about singing?

SARAH, PLAIN AND TALL

JOURNAL WRITING: Discussion; Students Write

`C` Discuss the things Sarah told about herself in her letter.

`Sy` Have each student write a letter to the family to explain at least four things about himself or herself and ask any questions he or she might have.

CHAPTER 2

VOCABULARY:

enclosing	flounder	pesky	shingles
envelope	fogbound	prefer	stalls

PREREADING DISCUSSION: Students Write

`Ap/ An` What questions would you want to ask Sarah? Write them in your journal. Read to find out if any of your questions are answered in this chapter.

POSTREADING DISCUSSION: Teacher Writes On Board

`An` List your questions about Sarah that were answered in the chapter.

`An/ Sy` Imagine that you are Sarah. Write a note to the family explaining how you will get to the farm and how they will recognize you.

CHAPTER 3

VOCABULARY:

chores	fetch	perfect	quilt	suspenders
clattered	hitched	preacher	slick	woodchuck

PREREADING DISCUSSION: Teacher Writes On Board

`Ap` If you were Sarah and you visited Jacob and his children, what presents would you give Anna and Caleb and why? (List the responses.)

POSTREADING DISCUSSION: Teacher Writes On Board

`An` How were your gift ideas similar to and different from Sarah's gift ideas?

JOURNAL WRITING: Students Write

`Sy` Imagine you are Caleb or Anna. Write a paragraph describing how you feel about your present.

SARAH, PLAIN AND TALL

CHAPTER 4

VOCABULARY:

C | conch   paddock   razor clam   roamer   rustle   scallop

PREREADING DISCUSSION:

An | Ask the students to find clues why Sarah might stay.

POSTREADING DISCUSSION: Teacher Writes On Board

C | Discuss the clues. *(Clues- Sarah said "winter" when talking about dry flowers. Sarah said "later" when spreading Caleb's curls for the birds.)*

JOURNAL WRITING: Students Write

Ap | On another piece of paper, list reasons why Sarah might stay or leave.

CHAPTER 5

VOCABULARY:

C | canvas   coarse   lantern   mound   windmill
      charcoal   dune   mica   turkey buzzard

PREREADING DISCUSSION: Students Draw

An | What kinds of pictures might Sarah draw and send to her brother in Maine?

Ap | Draw a picture in your journal that you think Sarah might draw.

POSTREADING DISCUSSION:

An | How is your picture similar to and different from any of Sarah's pictures?

Ev | Explain why you think Sarah would have drawn "your picture."

JOURNAL WRITING: Teacher Reads; Discussion; Students Write

Read aloud the passage beginning, "'In Maine', said Sarah, 'there are rock cliffs...,'" and ending with, "'...slide down the dune into the water'."

Ev | Have the students write descriptions in their journals of the pictures they drew.

SARAH, PLAIN AND TALL

CHAPTER 6

VOCABULARY:

C				
chanted	gullies	sputtering	streaming	treaded
collapsed	reins	startled	sums	tumbleweeds

PREREADING DISCUSSION: Teacher Writes On Board

An What do you think happens on the prairie and the seashore during the winter?

POSTREADING DISCUSSION: Teacher Writes On Board

C Which of the ideas that were listed before the chapter was read and mentioned in the chapter? (Circle listed responses.) Discuss other sources from which you could get information about winters in these places.

JOURNAL WRITING: Students Write

Sy Use information from the lists on board, the story, and other sources to write a description of winter on the prairie or the seashore.

CHAPTER 7

VOCABULARY:

C			
bantam	greens	squawk	Tennessee
dandelions	primly	streak	whicker

PREREADING DISCUSSION: Students Draw In Journal

An Sarah receives some presents from a neighbor in this chapter. Draw and label other presents you think she might receive. Be prepared to support your ideas.

POSTREADING DISCUSSION:

K What were the presents Maggie brought for Sarah? (Answer: three red banty chickens and plants for a garden.) Why do you think she chose these things?

JOURNAL WRITING: Students Write

Discuss the students' ideas for suitable presents for Sarah.

Ap/ An Have each student write about why one of his or her gift ideas would have been a good choice for Sarah.

SARAH, PLAIN AND TALL

CHAPTER 8

VOCABULARY:

argument	eerie	pungent	steady	weary
carpenter	huddled	squall	stubbornly	wisps

PREREADING DISCUSSION:

 Discuss things that some people say boys or girls cannot do. Do you agree with these statements? Why or why not?

POSTREADING DISCUSSION:

 In what other way could Sarah have handled the situation?

JOURNAL WRITING: Teacher Reads; Discussion; Students Write

Read aloud the passage beginning, "At dawn there was a sudden sound…," and ending with, "Like the sea."

 Have the students write about other things that might have been in the scene and how the characters felt.

CHAPTER 9

VOCABULARY:

complained	groom	peering	scuttling	stern
damaged	murmured	promise	squinted	wailed

PREREADING DISCUSSION:

 Is Sarah going to leave or stay? Explain your response.

POSTREADING DISCUSSION:

 Discuss the meaning of Sarah's statement: "I always will miss my old home, but the truth is, I will miss you more."

 Have students give examples of this from their own lives.

SARAH, PLAIN AND TALL

JOURNAL WRITING: Students Write And Draw

Ap Pretend that you are Anna or Caleb. Write a letter and draw a picture for Sarah to express your feelings about her decision to stay.

CULMINATING ACTIVITIES

POSTREADING DISCUSSION:

An What words could be used to describe each of the following characters: Caleb, Anna, Papa, Sarah?

Ev What were your most and least favorite parts of the book?

STORY FRAME: Discussion; Students Read; Teacher Writes On Board; Students Fill In Story Frames

C Have the students "fill in" the characters and setting, discuss the plot, and review the fill-in summaries in their individual guides to construct ideas for their book summaries. Have the class brainstorm major events in the story. As a group, consolidate statements and ideas until everyone has an understanding of the story summary. After the students fill in the summary sections of their story frames, discuss the responses.

JOURNAL WRITING: Students Write

Ev Have each student choose one of the following culminating activities:

•What would have happened if Sarah left?

•Describe a typical day on the farm and include details of what everyone does.

•Write a newspaper article about Papa and Sarah's wedding.

•Write a poem about the prairie and/or the seashore.

•Keep a diary for one of the characters.

SARAH, PLAIN AND TALL

MATH

CALCULATING DISTANCE:

Have the students use the scale on a map to calculate the distance Sarah traveled on her journey to the farm. Then have them calculate how long it would have taken her to make the journey in a wagon or on a train.

SOCIAL STUDIES

MAPPING:

Instruct the students to plot Sarah's travels from Maine to the plains.

COMPARATIVE STUDIES:

Conduct a study of the life-styles of people living in Maine and people living on farms in the plains.

SCIENCE

COMPARATIVE ECOSYSTEMS:

Have the students study the plains and the seashore. Then ask each student to compare and contrast wildlife and living conditions in each location.

FINE ARTS

SHELLS:

Conduct a study of seashells. Let the students bring shell collections to class.

In The Year
Of The Boar
And Jackie Robinson

...and it's the bottom of the ninth, bases loaded with...

JANUARY — Chinese New Year

K   1. What were the girls' two names? _____

Sy   2. On another piece of paper, draw the stamp that might have been on the letters.

K   3. Who was Bandit's best friend? _____

K   4. What does Bandit say to make you think there had been a war? _____

_____

An   5. Why do you think the servant was called "Awaiting Marriage"? _____

_____

An   6. On another piece of paper, write words to "explain" the following characters: Awaiting Marriage, Fourth Cousin, Precious Coins, Grandfather.

K   7. What would the Year of the Boar bring? _____

Ap   8. On another piece of paper, draw a picture of Grand-grand Auntie as Grand-grand Uncle might have done. Then describe the picture.

An   9. On another piece of paper, tell what you think happened to make Grand-grand Uncle and Grand-grand Auntie stop talking to each other for sixty years.

K   10. What official name did Bandit choose? _____

An   11. Why do you think the chapter was called "Chinese New Year"? _____

_____

C   12. On another piece of paper, draw and label three main events of the chapter.

FEBRUARY — A Journey of Ten Thousand Miles

C   **13.** How did Shirley feel while she was crossing the ocean? _____

_____

C   **14.** On another piece of paper, explain the meaning of this statement: "At last it was the hour when their year-long separation would end."

K   **15.** What city in New York was Shirley's new home and by what name did she call it? _____

C   **16.** On another piece of paper, draw a picture of the inside of Shirley's new home.

K   **17.** How was the kitchen in Shirley's new home different from the one in China?

_____

_____

An   **18.** What do you think the orange noodles that came out of a can were? Why?

_____

_____

Ev   **19.** Why do you think the chapter was called, "A Journey of Ten Thousand Miles"? _____

_____

C   **20.** On another piece of paper, draw and label three main events of this chapter.

MARCH — China's Little Ambassador

K 21. Could Shirley speak or understand English? _____

C 22. "On the day she was born, she was one year old. And two months later, upon the new year, she was two." How old is Shirley in American years? _____

Ap 23. How old are you in Chinese years? _____

K 24. In what grade did they place Shirley? _____

Ap 25. In what grade should Shirley have been placed? _____

C 26. On another piece of paper, explain what Mother meant when she said, "Upon your shoulders rests the reputation of all Chinese."

Ev 27. How would you feel if someone said that to you? _____
_____

Ap 28. "Suddenly, the principal shut one eye, the right one, then opened it again." Do this. What was the principal doing and why? _____
_____
_____

Ap 29. Shirley "...shut and opened both eyes. Twice." Do this. What was Shirley trying to say by doing this? _____
_____

C 30. Why do you think the chapter was called "China's Little Ambassador"? _____
_____

Sy 31. What other title would you give this chapter and why? _____
_____

C 32. On another piece of paper, draw and label three main events of the chapter.

APRIL — A Hungry Ghost

K 33. Why did Shirley think that her classmates ignored her? _____

_____

K 34. Circle the statement that Shirley thought was true.

She could speak only a few words of English.

She was a coward.

She was stupid.

She was lonely.

Sy 35. On another piece of paper, describe a time when you felt like Shirley.

Ev 36. On another piece of paper, tell how your favorite game is played.

An 37. How is "stoop ball" the same as and different from your favorite game?_____

_____

_____

C 38. After reciting her poem, the class laughed. What does it mean, "...soon she stood like a forlorn scarecrow under the pelting rain"? _____

_____

_____

C 39. What kind of lessons did Shirley take? _____

_____

Ev. 40. Why do you think the chapter was called "A Hungry Ghost"? _____

_____

_____

Sy 41. What other title would you give this chapter and why? _____

_____

_____

K 42. On another piece of paper, draw and label three main events of this chapter.

MAY — Two Black Eyes and Wispy Whiskers

C 43. Explain the following statement on another piece of paper: "The good deed and the height made her feel superior to the boys and girls playing stickball in the yard."

K 44. What compliment did Shirley's teacher give her? _____
_____

C 45. Why did Shirley blush upon hearing the compliment? _____
_____

K 46. When Mable walked up to Shirley, why didn't Shirley move? _____
_____

Ev 47. Why do you think Mable talked to Shirley? _____

C 48. What did Mable do for Shirley? _____
_____

Sy 49. When Shirley came into home base, everyone chanted. Make up your own chant for Shirley. (Include the name of Jackie Robinson.) _____
_____
_____
_____
_____

K 50. What did Mable teach Shirley on Saturday and Sunday? _____
_____

C 51. On another piece of paper, explain what Grandfather meant when he said, "Good can be bad. Bad can be good. Sadness can be happiness. Joy, sorrow."

C 52. Why do you think the chapter was called "Two Black Eyes and Wispy Whiskers"? _____

Sy 53. What other title would you give this chapter and why? _____
_____

C 54. On another piece of paper, draw and label three main events of this chapter.

JUNE — I Pledge A Lesson To The Frog

An 55. On another piece of paper, explain how the pledge of allegiance that Shirley said is the same as or different from the actual pledge of allegiance?

K 56. Why did the kids call Shirley "teacher's dog" and "apple shiner"? _____

_____

_____

K 57. What was Shirley's question for the teacher? _____

_____

_____

C 58. Why do you think this chapter is titled "I Pledge a Lesson to the Frog"? _____

_____

_____

Sy 59. What other title would you give this chapter and why? _____

_____

_____

C 60. Draw and label three main events in this chapter.

© 1990 by Incentive Publications, Inc., Nashville, TN.

JULY — Toscanini Takes A Walk

C   **61.** On another piece of paper, explain the following statement: "Without stickball, the school yard had an eerie look as desolate as Chungking during an air raid."

K   **62.** On another piece of paper, list the things Shirley would do if she were on vacation in China during vacation.

Ap   **63.** What things do you do during summer vacation? _____
_____

C   **64.** Why had writing in Chinese become such a chore for Shirley? _____
_____

K   **65.** What would Shirley do during the summer? _____
_____

Ev   **66.** When Jackie Robinson's sixteen game hitting streak ended, Shirley blamed herself. Do you agree or disagree with Shirley? Why? _____
_____

An   **67.** How is Shirley's parents' reaction the same as or different from your parents' reaction to TV? _____
_____

K   **68.** What did Shirley volunteer to do for Senora? _____

C   **69.** On another piece of paper, explain Senora's problem.

K   **70.** How did Shirley help Senora with her problem? _____
_____

Ev   **71.** Why do you think this chapter was titled "Toscanini Takes a Walk"? _____
_____

Sy   **72.** What other title would you give this chapter and why? _____
_____

C   **73.** On another piece of paper, draw and label three main events of this chapter.

AUGUST — Monsters

C 74. On another piece of paper, explain the following statement: "A paste of Chinese herbs concocted by Mother had magically coaxed sore gums to adopt the twenty-eight intruders fashioned by the dentist."

K 75. What was the surprise? _____

_____

C 76. On another piece of paper, draw and label the presents Father made for each tenant.

C 77. What was Shirley doing when the lights went out? _____

_____

C 78. On another piece of paper, explain the following statement about Shirley's trip to the furnace room: "Her legs felt like spaghetti out of a can."

K 89. What did Shirley think the walls felt like? Why? _____

_____

K 90. When Father came to help turn the lights on, what did Shirley notice about the walls? _____

_____

C 91. Why do you think the chapter is titled "Monsters"? _____

_____

_____

C 92. On another piece of paper, draw and label three main events of this chapter.

SEPTEMBER — Secrets

K 93. What happened to Toscanini? _____

An 94. Think of American expressions that do not have Chinese translations (such as "Gee whiz," and "What's up?").

K 95. Whom did Shirley meet in this chapter and what did her new friend look like?_____
_____

K 96. How did Emily describe herself? _____

An 97. How would you describe yourself? _____

C 98. What two secrets did Shirley keep in this chapter? _____
_____

K 99. What did Shirley do to make baby-sitting easier? _____
_____

C 100. On another piece of paper, explain the following statement: "This time when the dimes dropped, the sound was hollow. Counterfeit."

K 101. How was Emily going to help Shirley replace buttons with dimes?_____
_____

C 102. On another piece of paper, explain the following statement: "Things thoughtlessly done are never so easily undone."

C 103. Why do you think the chapter is titled "Secrets"? _____
_____

Sy 104. What other title would you give this chapter and why? _____
_____

C 105. On another piece of paper, draw and label three main events of this chapter.

© 1990 by Incentive Publications, Inc., Nashville, TN.

OCTOBER — The World Series

K 106. What made Mr. P special during the world series? _____

_____

C 107. On another piece of paper, explain the following statement: "This was no game. This was war."

Ev 108. Have you ever felt like Shirley about any kind of game? Why? _____

_____

An 109. Why do you think Tommy said, "De Bums played like amateurs"? _____

_____

Ev 110. Why didn't anyone speak to Tommy after he made that statement? _____

_____

C 111. On another piece of paper, explain what Tommy meant when he said that the Dodgers "...got as much chance as a guppy swallowing a whale."

C 112. On another piece of paper, explain the following statement: "Forgetting thirty-nine generations of Confucian breeding, Shirley hugged anyone in reach."

Ev 113. Why do you think the chapter is titled "The World Series"? _____

_____

C 114. On another piece of paper, draw and label three main events of this chapter.

NOVEMBER — Moon Cakes Without Grandfather

K **115.** What did Shirley and her parents watch from their kitchen? _____

_____

_____

K **116.** What did Grandpa send and why? _____

_____

_____

_____

K **117.** What was the problem with the family? _____

_____

_____

Ev **118.** Why do you think the chapter is titled "Moon Cakes Without Grandfather"?

_____

_____

_____

_____

C **119.** On another piece of paper, draw and label three main events of this chapter.

DECEMBER — A Star-Spangled Christmas

K 120. What was Shirley's turkey costume made of? _____

K 121. What did Mrs. Rappaport say that the class would hold? _____

C 122. On another piece of paper, draw a picture of Shirley's tree at home. Label what is hanging from the branches.

K 123. What news did Shirley's mother tell her the night before and what does it mean? _____

_____

K 124. On another piece of paper, list the American and Chinese things Shirley would teach her new brother or sister.

K 125. Why did Shirley think that Mable and Emily should be on stage? _____

_____

Ev 126. Why do you think Shirley was the best choice? _____

Ap 127. On another piece of paper, write what you would have said when presenting the key of your school to Jackie Robinson if you were Shirley.

C 128. On another piece of paper, explain what Jackie Robinson meant when he said, "Remember what I said in my talk — excel."

K 129. Why couldn't Shirley be president of the United States? _____

_____

C 130. Who in Shirley's family could be president and why? _____

_____

Ev 131. On another piece of paper, explain the last paragraph of the book.

IN THE YEAR OF THE BOAR AND JACKIE ROBINSON

1. Make a family tree for your "clan." Write a brief sentence below each person's name to describe that person.

2. Make a diorama of your favorite part of the story.

3. Practice writing Chinese characters for the numbers 1-10 and the months of the year. Teach others in your class to do the same.

4. Dress as a character in the book and explain what happens to you in the story.

5. Draw six pictures to illustrate American life experiences Shirley had. Write a sentence about each picture.

6. Write a report about Jackie Robinson.

7. Draw a map of China and the United States. Chart Shirley's voyage and her train trip to Brooklyn.

8. Design a poster to advertise the book. Show it to the class and convince them to read it.

9. Tape-record an interview between Shirley and Jackie Robinson.

10. Make a scrapbook for your favorite sports team. Explain its contents.

11. Tape-record the story Shirley told in the chapter titled "November — Moon Cakes Without Grandfather." Tell the story slowly and with meaning as Grandfather would.

IN THE YEAR OF THE BOAR AND JACKIE ROBINSON

PRELIMINARY ACTIVITIES

GETTING READY TO READ: Discussion

K | Who is the author? *Bette Bao Lord*

An | What do you think the story is about? *answers will vary*

PREREADING DISCUSSION: Teacher Writes On Board

Ev | How would you feel if you had to move to another country?

JOURNAL WRITING: Students Write

Ev | What would you be afraid of and excited about if you were moving?

JANUARY — Chinese New Year

VOCABULARY:

C |

ancestors	barbarian	delicacies	matriarch	preference
applauded	decreed	festooned	misdeed	relented

PREREADING DISCUSSION:

Ap | How does your family celebrate holidays? Read to find out how the main character celebrates a special Chinese holiday.

POSTREADING DISCUSSION: Teacher Writes On Board

Ap | How was Bandit/Shirley's way of celebrating Chinese New Year similar to and different from the way you celebrate holidays?

JOURNAL WRITING: Students Write

Sy | Write a letter to your father from Bandit/Shirley's point of view to explain your feelings about moving and your new name.

FEBRUARY — A Journey of Ten Thousand Miles

VOCABULARY:

C |

attained	burrowed	faltered	linger	solemn
bewitched	clutched	immigration	ogled	torrential
boasted	customs	launder	relic	writhed

IN THE YEAR OF THE BOAR AND JACKIE ROBINSON

PREREADING DISCUSSION:

`An` How will America differ from China? Read to find out how Shirley's experiences in Brooklyn are different from those she had in China.

POSTREADING DISCUSSION: Students Skim Chapter; Teacher Writes On Board

`An` How were things in America different from Shirley's home in China?

JOURNAL WRITING: Students Write

`An` List your favorite foods and tell how you think Shirley would describe each.

MARCH — China's Little Ambassador

VOCABULARY:

`C`
| curiosity | escapade | gesture | introduced | quizzical |
| embarrassing | foreign | gurgling | obediently | trembling |

PREREADING DISCUSSION:

`C` What is an ambassador? Read to find out how Shirley acts as an ambassador.

POSTREADING DISCUSSION: Students Skim Chapter; Teacher Writes On Board

`An` How was Shirley a good ambassador for her country?

JOURNAL WRITING: Students Write

`Sy` Explain how you would be a good ambassador for the United States.

APRIL — A Hungry Ghost

VOCABULARY:

`C`
| bulged | fleetingly | groaned | protruded | scientifically |
| dreaded | grimaced | humiliated | revolted | somersaulted |

PREREADING DISCUSSION:

`Ev` How do you act when you're lonely? Read to find out how Shirley handles it.

POSTREADING DISCUSSION: Teacher Writes On Board

`Ev` What can Shirley do to feel less lonely?

IN THE YEAR OF THE BOAR AND JACKIE ROBINSON

JOURNAL WRITING: Students Write

Sy | Write a letter to Shirley to make her feel better.

MAY — Two Black Eyes and Wispy Whiskers

VOCABULARY:

C | compliments   hesitated   intimidated   reverent   superior
confident   interrogate   persuasive   rookie   uncivilized

PREREADING DISCUSSION: Teacher Writes On Board

An | If someone hurt you, would you tell? List reasons why you would or wouldn't tell. Shirley finds herself in this predicament. Read to find out what she does.

POSTREADING DISCUSSION: Teacher Writes On Board

Ev | What do you think would have happened if Shirley had told about Mable hitting her? Why? ("Chain" the responses.)

JOURNAL WRITING: Students Write

Sy | Write about what would have happened if Shirley had told on Mable.

JUNE — I Pledge a Lesson to the Frog

VOCABULARY:

C | beckoned   civics   crimson   proposal   victim

PREREADING DISCUSSION:

Ev | Who are your heroes? Read to see how Jackie Robinson becomes Shirley's hero.

POSTREADING DISCUSSION: Teacher Reads; Teacher Writes On Board

Read the passage beginning, "Jackie Robinson is the grandson of a slave, the son of a sharecropper, raised in poverty by a lone mother who took In ironing and washing," and ending, "She felt as if she had the power of ten tigers, as if she had grown as tall as the Statue of Liberty."

An | How is Shirley like Jackie Robinson? (List the responses.)

IN THE YEAR OF THE BOAR AND JACKIE ROBINSON

JOURNAL WRITING: Students Write

 An How are you like Jackie Robinson?

JULY — Toscanini Takes a Walk

VOCABULARY:

C | awkwardly   desolate   disposition   illustrious   mayhem   sultry

PREREADING DISCUSSION:

Ap What do you do during summer vacation? Shirley begins her summer vacation in this chapter. Read to find out how her summer compares to yours.

POSTREADING DISCUSSION: Teacher Writes On Board

An How is Shirley's summer vacation similar to and different from yours?

JOURNAL WRITING: Students Write

Sy If Shirley were your friend, what kinds of things would you do together during summer vacation? How would you help Shirley and how would she help you?

AUGUST — Monsters

VOCABULARY:

C
adept	figment	innards	pennant	suspicious
collided	imagination	meticulous	refrain	waxed
dungeon	infamous	obedient	spectator	

PREREADING DISCUSSION:

Ev Why are people sometimes afraid of the dark? Shirley has an experience in the dark in this chapter. Read to find out what it is.

POSTREADING DISCUSSION:

 Ev How would this chapter be different if Shirley had not volunteered to take care of the house while Senora Rodriquez went to see her daughter? ("Chain" the responses.)

IN THE YEAR OF THE BOAR AND JACKIE ROBINSON

JOURNAL WRITING: Teacher Reads; Students Write

Read the passage beginning, "The dungeon held no monster, but it was a beastly mess," and ending, "Fearing lizards and rats, cockroaches and snakes, Shirley hastened to her father's side."

Sy Describe a dark room in your house or garage in a scary way.

SEPTEMBER — Secrets

VOCABULARY:

C

account	customary	deposit	expensive	thrilled
bribing	counterfeit	essence	operating	valuable

PREREADING DISCUSSION:

Ev Is it right to keep a secret? Read to find out how Shirley handles a secret.

POSTREADING DISCUSSION: Teacher Writes On Board

Ev What would have happened if Shirley had told the secret?

JOURNAL WRITING: Teacher Reads; Students Write

Read the passage beginning, "She wanted to tell them all that was in her heart, but how do you express such feelings?" and ending, "But Shirley wanted to find a special way, her own way. What could it be?"

Sy If you were Shirley, how would you show your parents how you felt?

OCTOBER — The World Series

VOCABULARY:

C amateurs   banished   berserk   phenomenon

PREREADING DISCUSSION:

Ev What would a friend of yours have to do to be kicked out of the group? Something happens to cause one of the group to be ousted. Read to find out what it is.

IN THE YEAR OF THE BOAR AND JACKIE ROBINSON

POSTREADING DISCUSSION: Teacher Writes On Board

Ev | What was another way everyone could have dealt with Tommy?

JOURNAL WRITING: Students Write

Sy | Pretend you are Tommy and write why you acted the way you did in this chapter and how you felt about the way your friends treated you.

NOVEMBER — Moon Cakes Without Grandfather

VOCABULARY:

C |

| betrothed | crescent | filial | longevity | precisely |
| commemorate | decreed | implored | mystified | shivered |

PREREADING DISCUSSION:

Ev | When do you miss your family and relatives the most? Shirley and her parents miss their relatives in this chapter. Read to find out what they do.

POSTREADING DISCUSSION: Teacher Writes On Board

Read the passage beginning, "Long, long ago, there lived a most honorable man who owed much of his good fortune to the kindness of his friends," and ending, "She was wearing two gowns. One that belonged to the fisherman's wife. One that belonged to the filial daughter."

An | How was Shirley like the fisherman's wife and the filial daughter?

JOURNAL WRITING: Students Write

Sy | Pretend you are Shirley. Write a letter to Grandfather telling him about your mid-autumn festival celebration and your feelings.

DECEMBER — A Star-Spangled Christmas

VOCABULARY:

C |

| anticipation | dominated | futility | instinctively | swaggering |
| boa | expectant | ingenuity | studiously | transformation |

IN THE YEAR OF THE BOAR AND JACKIE ROBINSON

PREREADING DISCUSSION:

Ev If you found out you were going to get a new baby sister or brother, what kinds of things would you plan to do for him or her? Shirley's mother tells her some good news in this chapter. Read to find out what Shirley plans to do about it.

POSTREADING DISCUSSION: Teacher Writes On Board

C Jackie Robinson said one should excel: "For some day you will all hold the keys to making America the greatest country in the world." What are some ways to accomplish what Jackie Robinson is talking about? (List the responses.)

JOURNAL WRITING: Students Write

 Write about how you plan to excel and make a difference in the world.

CULMINATING ACTIVITIES

POSTREADING DISCUSSION:

An How has Shirley changed? Would you want Shirley for a friend? Why or why not? What is your favorite/least favorite part of the book? Why?

STORY FRAME: Discussion; Students Read; Teacher Writes On Board; Students Fill In Story Frames

C Have the students fill in the characters and setting on their story frames. Discuss the plot and then have the students review their chapter fill-in summaries. Ask the class to brainstorm major events in the story (list these on the board). Consolidate statements and ideas until everyone has an understanding of the summary. Then have the students fill in the summary sections of their story frames.

JOURNAL WRITING: Students Write

 Have each student choose one of the following culminating activities:

- Write a diary for Shirley with one entry for each month in the year.
- How would the story be different if Shirley were born in the United States?
- Write a newspaper story about Jackie Robinson's appearance at P.S. 8.
- From Jackie Robinson's point of view, write about your experience of receiving the key of the school from Shirley.

IN THE YEAR OF THE BOAR AND JACKIE ROBINSON

MATH

MEASUREMENT/GRAPHING:

Have the students measure how far each of them can hit and throw a baseball. Graph the results.

SOCIAL STUDIES

SIMILARITIES/DIFFERENCES:

Have the students research Chinese culture and keep a running chart of similarities and differences between Chinese culture and American culture.

CURRENT EVENTS:

Ask the students to follow current news stories about China. Discuss the stories as a class.

CHINESE HOLIDAYS:

Celebrate Chinese New Year or Moon Festival as a class.

SCIENCE

EXPERIMENT:

Have the students use a scientific method to fly kites. Instruct each student to do the following:

- Design a kite and fly it. Record the results.
- Modify the kite and record the modification and your hypothesis of how it will fly.
- Fly the kite again and record the results and your conclusion about the kite's design.

FINE ARTS

COLLAGE:

Have the students cut out pictures and words related to favorite sports heroes/heroines and paste them on poster board to make a collage. Or, have the students make a collage based on a Chinese theme.

WATERCOLOR:

Have the students practice writing the Chinese characters for each month (these may be found in the book) with watercolors and paintbrushes.

KITES:

Let the students design kites on paper and/or make kites to fly outdoors.

Mrs. Frisby And The Rats Of NIMH

CHAPTER 1 — The Sickness of Timothy Frisby

Rewrite sentences 1 - 3 on another piece of paper. Look up the underlined words in the dictionary.

C   1. They moved into the winter house when food got too <u>scarce</u>.

     2. The hollows made two <u>spacious</u> rooms.

C   3. The potatoes had been thawed and refrozen so that they <u>acquired</u> a slimy <u>texture</u> and a <u>rancid</u> taste.

C   4. On another piece of paper, briefly describe all of the characters in the chapter.

K   5. What did Mrs. Frisby think happened to the animal who stored all the food?

_____

An   6. On another piece of paper, draw pictures of the three main events in this chapter and label them in order.

Sy   7. On another piece of paper, write a summary of this chapter.

CHAPTER 2 — Mr. Ages

Rewrite sentences 8 - 10 on another piece of paper. Look up the underlined words in the dictionary.

C   8. Timothy <u>obviously</u> could not wait until the next day.

C   9. The cat <u>stalked</u> those grounds <u>relentlessly</u>.

C   10. Her <u>progress</u> was almost completely noiseless.

K   11. On another piece of paper, list the raw materials Mr. Ages collected.

Sy   12. What different title would you give this chapter and why? _____

_____

An   13. On another piece of paper, draw pictures of the three main events in this chapter and label them in order.

C   14. On another piece of paper, write a summary of this chapter.

CHAPTER 3 — The Crow and the Cat

Rewrite sentences 15 - 17 on another piece of paper. Look up the underlined words in the dictionary.

C 15. Dragon's name turned into an <u>apt</u> one.

C 16. He gave a high, <u>strangled</u> scream.

C 17. At length she came <u>abreast</u> of the barn.

Ap 18. On another piece of paper, draw and describe Dragon.

Sy 19. On another piece of paper, write a story you think Timothy might have made up for Cynthia.

Sy 20. Draw a Christmas package from which the silver string could have come. Draw and label what you think was inside the package.

An 21. On another piece of paper, draw pictures of the three main events in this chapter and label them in order.

Sy 22. On another piece of paper, write a summary of this chapter.

CHAPTER 4 — Mr. Fitzgibbon's Plow

Rewrite sentences 23 - 25. Look up the underlined words in the dictionary.

C 23. The other children were waiting, frightened, sad, and <u>subdued</u>.

C 24. He woke up twice, and the second time he wasn't <u>delirious</u>.

C 25. The next morning, as <u>predicted</u>, Timothy's fever was lower.

Sy 26. On another piece of paper, describe a time when you were sick like Timothy.

C 27. On another piece of paper, explain what this statement means: "Mrs. Frisby could not quite get rid of a nagging worry that kept flickering in her mind."

C 28. On another piece of paper, describe Mrs. Frisby's problem in this chapter.

Ev 29. On another piece of paper, tell how Mrs. Frisby can solve this problem.

An 30. On another piece of paper, draw pictures of the three main events in this chapter and label them in order.

Sy 31. On another piece of paper, write a summary of this chapter.

CHAPTER 5 — Five Days

Rewrite sentences 32 - 34 on another piece of paper. Look up the underlined words in the dictionary.

C   **32.** She discovered a <u>convenient</u> knot hole where she could hide.

C   **33.** Mrs. Fitzgibbon backed the tractor out of the <u>cluttered</u> shed and kept the motor <u>idling</u>.

C   **34.** Five days, although a <u>respite</u>, was too short.

Ev   **35.** After seeing the tractor, Mrs. Frisby thought of going back to Mr. Ages for advice. On another piece of paper, tell what else Mrs. Frisby could do to help.

An   **36.** On another piece of paper, tell why the cat Dragon did not chase Mrs. Frisby.

Sy   **37.** On another piece of paper, write a summary of this chapter.

CHAPTER 6 — A Favor From Jeremy

Rewrite sentences 38 - 40 on another piece of paper. Look up the underlined words in the dictionary.

C   **38.** The mild breeze carried the <u>moist essence</u> of early spring.

C   **39.** A black object <u>plummeted</u> from the sky.

C   **40.** It depends on what kind of <u>humor</u> he's in.

Ev   **41.** Whom do you think Jeremy was collecting shiny things for and why? _____

_____

Sy   **42.** On another piece of paper, write about a favor you did for someone.

Ev   **43.** Do you think Jeremy's favor will help Mrs. Frisby? Why or why not? _____

_____

_____

Sy   **44.** On another piece of paper, write a summary of the chapter.

CHAPTER 7 — The Owl

Rewrite sentences 45 - 47 on another piece of paper. Look up the underlined words in the dictionary.

C   **45.** Timothy had not been told about the <u>expedition</u>.

C   **46.** She felt the <u>surge</u> of power as the wings beat against the air.

C   **47.** Mrs. Frisby was rather ashamed of her <u>ignorance</u>.

C   **48.** On another piece of paper, explain what this statement means: "Jeremy appeared when the last thumbnail of sun winked out over the mountains beyond the meadow."

Ev   **49.** On another piece of paper, explain how you would feel if you were Mrs. Frisby.

Ev   **50.** On another piece of paper, tell how would you feel about speaking to the owl in his house if you were Mrs. Frisby.

Sy   **51.** On another piece of paper, write a summary of the chapter.

CHAPTER 8 — Go to the Rats

Rewrite sentences 52 - 54 on another piece of paper. Look up the underlined words in the dictionary.

C   **52.** Your house will <u>inevitably</u> be turned up by the plow.

C   **53.** There is no <u>feasible</u> way to prevent this.

C   **54.** He gave an <u>agitated</u> flutter of his wings.

K   **55.** On another piece of paper, write the advice the owl first gave Mrs. Frisby and the advice he gave her when he learned she was the widow of Jonathan Frisby.

Sy   **56.** On another piece of paper, describe something you got so attached to that you didn't want to leave it or throw it away.

C   **57.** What does "in the lee" mean? _____

_____

Sy   **58.** On another piece of paper, write a summary of the chapter.

CHAPTER 9 — In the Rosebush

Rewrite sentences 59 - 61. Look up the underlined words in the dictionary.

C   **59.** She paused a moment to <u>eavesdrop</u> on their conversation.

C   **60.** Mrs. Frisby tried to sound as <u>casual</u> as she could.

C   **61.** One did not <u>prowl</u> in their <u>domain</u>.

An   **62.** On another piece of paper, list what you think the children had for dinner.

Ap   **63.** On another piece of paper, draw what you think the inside of the rosebush looked like. Include the clearing, doorway, and rat.

An   **64.** On another piece of paper, draw pictures of the three main events in this chapter and label them in order.

Sy   **65.** On another piece of paper, write a summary of this chapter.

CHAPTER 10 — Brutus

Rewrite sentences 66 - 68. Look up the underlined words in the dictionary.

C   **66.** She was turned back so <u>abruptly</u> at the end.

C   **67.** He sounded <u>cordial</u> enough.

C   **68.** Justin looked at her <u>casually</u>.

Ap   **69.** On another piece of paper, draw Brutus as you imagine him to be.

Sy   **70.** What different title would you give this chapter and why? _____

_____

An   **71.** On another piece of paper, draw pictures of the three main events in this chapter and label them in order.

Sy   **72.** On another piece of paper, write a summary of this chapter.

CHAPTER 11 — In the Library

Rewrite sentences 73 - 75. Look up the underlined words in the dictionary.

C 73. Ahead she could hear the <u>scuffle</u> of Justin's footsteps.

C 74. Mrs. Frisby could now <u>discern</u> the tunnel's shape and direction.

C 75. A tiny bulb had been <u>recessed</u> in a hole.

An 76. What new thing did Mrs. Frisby encounter with which she had not had a previous experience? _____

Ap 77. What two things did Nicodemus have that made him look different? Draw and label them on another piece of paper.

K 78. What was the reason for the rats' meeting? _____

Sy 79. On another piece of paper, write a summary of this chapter.

CHAPTER 12 — Isabella

Rewrite sentences 80 - 82. Look up the underlined words in the dictionary.

C 80. She had an <u>overwhelming</u> desire to look around.

C 81. They had all been friendly but <u>explicit</u>.

C 82. She was not there to <u>pry</u> but to get help.

K 83. On another piece of paper, write everything that was on the chalkboard.

C 84. On another piece of paper, write a brief description of the three new characters introduced in this chapter.

C 85. What was the grain room probably used for? _____

Sy 86. On another piece of paper, write a summary of the chapter.

CHAPTER 13 — A Powder for Dragon

Rewrite sentences 87 - 89. Look up the underlined words in the dictionary.

C 87. He looked <u>efficient</u>.

C 88. Nicodemus took the reading glass from his <u>satchel</u>.

C 89. You will forgive the glass and the <u>scrutiny</u>.

K 90. What did Mrs. Frisby volunteer to do? _____

K 91. On another piece of paper, tell what happened to two other people who attempted to do what Mrs. Frisby volunteered to do.

Sy 92. What different title would you give this chapter and why? _____

_____

An 93. On another piece of paper, draw pictures of the three main events in this chapter and label them in order.

Sy 94. On another piece of paper, write a summary of the chapter.

CHAPTER 14 — The Marketplace

Rewrite sentences 95 - 97 on another piece of paper. Look up the underlined word in the dictionary.

C 95. "I had forgotten," said Justin <u>contritely</u>.

C 96. It was something <u>vaguely</u> remembered from what Jonathan had told her.

C 97. The fisherman brought crabs, oysters, bass, and <u>flounders</u>.

Ap 98. On another piece of paper, draw eight kinds of food found at the Farmer's Market and label each.

Ev 99. Why do you think the rats were caught? _____

Sy 100. On another piece of paper, write a summary of the chapter.

CHAPTER 15 — In the Cage

Rewrite sentences 101 - 103 on another piece of paper. Look up the underlined words in the dictionary.

C 101. They hauled it away to the city <u>incinerator</u>.

C 102. I was firmly and <u>inextricably</u> caught.

C 103. Into this our net was <u>thrust</u>.

Ev 104. Where do you think Jenner heard the word "laboratory"? _____

_____

Ev 105. On another piece of paper, describe what it would be like to be in a cage.

Sy 106. On another piece of paper, write a summary of the chapter.

CHAPTER 16 — The Maze

Rewrite sentences 107 - 109 on another piece of paper. Look up the underlined words in the dictionary.

C 107. Dr. Schultz was a <u>neurologist</u>.

C 108. Through a <u>concealed</u> opening, George had been watching everything I did.

C 109. When you've lived in a cage, you can't bear not to run, even if what you are running toward is an <u>illusion</u>.

C 110. On another piece of paper, briefly describe Dr. Schultz, George, and Julie.

Ap 111. On another piece of paper, draw what you think the maze looked like and label each part. Include the electric shocks and the trap at the end.

Ev 112. Why do you think Julie and Dr. Schultz didn't pick up Justin? Why did they watch him? _____

Sy 113. On another piece of paper, write a summary of the chapter.

CHAPTER 17 — A Lesson In Reading

Rewrite sentences 114 - 116. Look up the underlined words in the dictionary.

C   114. He <u>submitted</u> <u>meekly</u> enough.

C   115. He had examined the air <u>ducts</u>.

C   116. Justin learned he would wander around without <u>incurring</u> any anger or injury.

Ap   117. On another piece of paper, describe in your own words what the letters "R," "A," and "T" look like.

Sy   118. On another piece of paper, write another sign you think might have been in the laboratory that the rats could have read.

Sy   119. On another piece of paper, write a summary of the chapter.

CHAPTER 18 — The Air Ducts

Rewrite sentences 120 - 122 on another piece of paper. Look up the underlined words in the dictionary.

C   120. Jenner was <u>astute</u> at that sort of thing.

C   121. They explored the shafts that <u>laced</u> like a <u>cubical</u> spiderweb.

C   122. Just as we were ending our meeting, a new <u>complication</u> arose.

Ap   123. On another piece of paper, draw and label the equipment they used to explore the duct.

An   124. On another piece of paper, draw and label three more things you would have used to explore the duct.

C   125. On another piece of paper, explain what Jenner meant when he said, "We aren't rats anymore."

Ev   126. On another piece of paper, tell where you would go if you were a rat who could read and why you would go there.

K   127. What happened to the mice who escaped with the rats? _____

_____

An   128. What do you think caused the wind in the air duct? _____

Sy   129. On another piece of paper, write a summary of this chapter.

CHAPTER 19 — The Boniface Estate

Rewrite sentences 130 - 132 on another piece of paper. Look up the underlined words in the dictionary.

C   **130.** The bolt was <u>secure</u>.

C   **131.** In the country there were <u>silos</u> filled with grain.

C   **132.** The other rats looked weak and <u>puny</u>.

Ev   **133.** On another piece of paper, draw and explain three dangerous times you think the rats might have had.

An   **134.** On another piece of paper, list three books you think the rats might have read.

Sy   **135.** On another piece of paper, write a summary of the chapter.

CHAPTER 20 — The Main Hall

Rewrite sentences 136 - 138 on another piece of paper. Look up the underlined words in the dictionary.

C   **136.** She had been so <u>engrossed</u> in the story.

C   **137.** The children were <u>skeptical</u> at first.

C   **138.** As she reached the <u>arched portal</u>, Brutus was standing guard.

Ev   **139.** Why do you think Mrs. Frisby didn't want to tell the children about their father's connection with the rats or the powder in Dragon's dish? _____

_____

Ap   **140.** On another piece of paper, tell what you think would have happened if Mrs. Frisby had kissed all of the children good-bye.

141. On another piece of paper, draw what you think the big room in the tunnel looked like and label the parts.

Sy   **142.** On another piece of paper, write a summary of this chapter.

CHAPTER 21 — The Toy Tinker

Rewrite sentences 143 - 145 on another piece of paper. Look up the underlined words in the dictionary.

C 143. We never spread diseases <u>intentionally</u>.

C 144. The <u>descendents</u> of early rats are prairie dogs.

C 145. After the prairies were overtaken, rats became <u>scavengers</u>.

Ap 146. On another piece of paper, describe rodents and draw rodent teeth. (Look up "rodent" in the encyclopedia for help.)

Ev 147. On another piece of paper, explain what probably caused the old man's death.

An 148. On another piece of paper, draw pictures of the three main events in this chapter and label them in order.

CHAPTER 22 — Thorn Valley

Rewrite sentences 149 - 151 on another piece of paper. Look up the underlined words in the dictionary.

C 149. It was closer than we planned to live to human <u>habitation</u>.

C 150. We put a <u>concealed</u> entrance there.

C 151. Our colony <u>thrived</u>.

Ap 152. On another piece of paper, draw and label the eight things that the truck contained to serve as the old man's living quarters.

C 153. On another piece of paper, explain what being in a "rat race" means.

C 154. How did Jenner feel about the plan? _____

_____

An 155. On another piece of paper, draw pictures of the three main events in this chapter and label them in order.

Sy 156. On another piece of paper, write a summary of this chapter.

CHAPTER 23 — Captured

Rewrite sentences 157 - 159 on another piece of paper. Look up the underlined word in the dictionary.

C   **157.** We felt strange <u>associating</u> with only the rats.

C   **158.** He didn't want to be <u>secretive</u>.

C   **159.** He <u>denounced</u> us as idiots and dreamers.

K   **160.** What were the two reasons they decided to destroy the machines? _____

_____

Ev   **161.** On another piece of paper, explain how you would have felt if you had put the powder in Dragon's dish.

Ap   **162.** On another piece of paper, explain what kind of cat food you think Mrs. Fitzgibbon gave Dragon and draw a picture of it.

C   **163.** On another piece of paper, describe Mrs. Frisby's problem in this chapter.

Sy   **164.** On another piece of paper, write a summary of the chapter.

CHAPTER 24 — Seven Dead Rats

Rewrite sentences 165 - 167 on another piece of paper. Look up the underlined words in the dictionary.

C   **165.** Billy slid a piece of cardboard beneath the <u>colander</u>.

C   **166.** Would Billy <u>plead</u> for a few more days?

C   **167.** The dead rats were <u>incinerated</u>.

An   **168.** On another piece of paper, list four chores you think the four hired hands do.

Sy   **169.** On another piece of paper, write an article entitled "Mechanized Rats Invade Hardware Store." Include who, what, where, why, and when.

Ev   **170.** On another piece of paper, tell why you think rabies was or was not the real reason the government got involved.

An   **171.** On another piece of paper, draw pictures of three main events in this chapter and label them in order.

CHAPTER 25 — Escape

Rewrite sentences 172 - 174 on another piece of paper. Look up the underlined words in the dictionary.

C   **172.** Dragon protested with the sleepiest of <u>whines</u>.

C   **173.** There were <u>vertical</u> bars on the cage.

C   **174.** You couldn't help it if they put you in a <u>defective</u> cage.

Ap   **175.** On another piece of paper, draw Mrs. Frisby in the cage.

Ap   **176.** On another piece of paper, draw and describe the scaffolding the rats used to move the cinder block.

An   **177.** On another piece of paper, draw pictures of the three main events in this chapter and label them in order.

CHAPTER 26 — At the Meeting

Rewrite sentences 178 - 180 on another piece of paper. Look up the underlined words in the dictionary.

C   **178.** There were two rats on <u>sentry</u> duty.

C   **179.** It could be a <u>coincidence</u>.

C   **180.** If they find an empty hole they might be <u>suspicious</u>.

C   **181.** On another piece of paper, tell what Mrs. Frisby intended to do in the house when they moved to their summer home.

C   **182.** List two ways the rats' plan had changed since the exterminators were coming. _____

_____

_____

_____

Sy   **183.** On another piece of paper, write a summary of the chapter.

CHAPTER 27 — The Doctor

Rewrite sentences 184 - 186 on another piece of paper. Look up the underlined words in the dictionary.

C   **184.** She could see the blackberry <u>bramble</u>.

C   **185.** There was a <u>conference</u> accompanied by <u>gestures</u>.

C   **186.** We'll be using <u>cyanide</u> and it's dangerous.

Ev   **187.** What do you think the rats were doing underground when the rosebush was bulldozed? _____

_____

Ev   **188.** Why do you think the men took the two dead rats? _____

_____

Sy   **189.** Write a summary of the chapter.

_____

_____

_____

_____

_____

_____

_____

_____

_____

_____

_____

_____

_____

_____

CHAPTER 28 — Epilogue

Rewrite sentences 190 - 192 on another piece of paper. Look up the underlined words in the dictionary.

C   **190.** The rats had <u>calculated</u> wisely.

C   **191.** The nearest <u>furrow</u> was more than two feet from her house.

C   **192.** The earthworms <u>writhed</u> in a frenzy to rebury themselves.

K   **193.** List the six crops the Fitzgibbons planted.

_____

_____

_____

_____

_____

_____

Ev   **194.** Who do you think the two dead rats were? Explain why. _____

_____

_____

Sy   **195.** What different title would you give this chapter and why? _____

_____

_____

An   **196.** On another piece of paper, draw pictures of the three main events in this chapter and label them in order.

Sy   **197.** On another piece of paper, write a summary of the chapter.

MRS. FRISBY AND THE RATS OF NIMH

1. Write a two-page report about rats or mice.

2. Design in colorful detail what the inside of the entire rat tunnel looked like. Label all the parts.

3. Bring a collection of at least ten shiny things Jeremy might like to class. Label each and display the collection.

4. Make a detailed diorama of the inside of Mrs. Frisby's home. Then explain it to someone.

5. Design the covers of at least five books you think the rats might have read. Be prepared to explain why you think the rats read them.

6. Describe another plan the rats might have had. Draw a map and write a page about it.

7. Draw a detailed and colorful map of where the rats went. Include all of the landmarks mentioned in the story (owl's tree, Fitzgibbon farm, Mrs. Frisby's house, etc.).

8. Pretend you are one of the characters in the story and write a diary of your experiences.

9. Make a model of the rat tunnel. Be prepared to describe it.

10. Write a three-part news article detailing the rats' story.

MRS. FRISBY AND THE RATS OF NIMH

PRELIMINARY ACTIVITIES

GETTING READY TO READ:

K Who is the author? *Robert C. O'Brien*

K Has the book won any awards? *Newbery Medal, Lewis Carroll Shelf Award*

Ap Where do you think the story takes places? *answers will vary*

Ap How many characters might the story have? *answers will vary*

An What do you think the story is about? *answers will vary*

PREREADING DISCUSSION:

Ev If a family member were sick and you had to move, what would you do?

JOURNAL WRITING: Discussion; Students Write

Ev If you had a problem, whose advice would you seek and why?

CHAPTER 1 — The Sickness of Timothy Frisby; CHAPTER 2 — Mr. Ages

VOCABULARY:

C

acquired	cinder block	obviously	rancid	stalked
authoritatively	delirious	pallet	relentlessly	tedious
botanical	hypochondriac	perspiration	scarce	texture
casually	loped	progress	spacious	tonic

PREREADING DISCUSSION: Teacher Writes On Board

An What's the difference between someone who is a hypochondriac and someone who actually is sick? (List the responses.)

POSTREADING DISCUSSION:

An Whom does Mr. Ages resemble? Why?

JOURNAL WRITING: Students Write

Sy Write about a time when you or someone in your family was sick.

MRS. FRISBY AND THE RATS OF NIMH

CHAPTER 3 — The Crow and the Cat; CHAPTER 4 — Mr. Fitzgibbon's Plow

VOCABULARY:

C

abreast	harrow	miserable	shrew	subdue
apt	illogical	predicted	solution	sympathetic
birdbrain	invariably	recover	strangled	

PREREADING DISCUSSION:

Ev What kind of dangers would Mrs. Frisby face on a farm? Read to find out what danger she faces in this chapter and how she solves her problem.

POSTREADING DISCUSSION: Teacher Writes On Board

An Tell how a tractor that starts is both a good and a bad thing.

JOURNAL WRITING: Students Write

Ev Write from Mrs. Frisby's point of view your thoughts upon hearing the tractor start. Then write about the same thing from Mr. Fitzgibbon's point of view.

CHAPTER 5 — Five Days; CHAPTER 6 — A Favor From Jeremy

VOCABULARY:

C

cluttered	essence	loft	plummeted	respite
conceal	hesitate	moist	remount	vantage
deliberately	humor	oddity		

PREREADING DISCUSSION:

An What reasons could Mr. Fitzgibbons have for starting the tractor? Read to find out why Mr. Fitzgibbons started the tractor and what problems this created for Mrs. Frisby.

An What reasons could Dragon the cat have for not chasing a mouse?

POSTREADING DISCUSSION:

Ev How might the owl help Mrs. Frisby? What could he do that Mr. Ages couldn't?

JOURNAL WRITING: Students Write

Sy Imagine that you are Mrs. Frisby and write what you want to say to the owl.

MRS. FRISBY AND THE RATS OF NIMH

CHAPTER 7 — The Owl; CHAPTER 8 — Go To the Rats

VOCABULARY:

affectionate	feasible	intrude	sentry	surge
agitated	ignorance	perceive	slither	talons
deference	inevitably	prediction	sonorous	updraft
expedition	instinctively	protrude	spacious	venture

PREREADING DISCUSSION:

What reasons might Mrs. Frisby have to be afraid of the owl? Read to find out what Mrs. Frisby's fears are and what she does about them.

POSTREADING DISCUSSION: Teacher Writes On Board

Read aloud the passage beginning, "I have lived in this tree, in this same hollow," and ending with, "One of these days, one of these years, the tree will fall, and when it does, if I am still alive, I will fall with it."

How are Mrs. Frisby's housing problem and the owl's housing problem similar and different? (List the responses.)

JOURNAL WRITING: Students Write

How would the story change if Jeremy had not taken Mrs. Frisby to see the owl?

CHAPTER 9 — In the Rosebush; CHAPTER 10 — Brutus

VOCABULARY:

abrupt	astonished	cordial	eavesdrop	timid
adjourned	casual	domain	guarantee	trespasses

JOURNAL WRITING: Students Write

Select one of the chapters and write a summary of it.

MRS. FRISBY AND THE RATS OF NIMH

PREREADING DISCUSSION:

Ev If you were Timothy, would you want to know about moving day? Why?

Ev If you were Mrs. Frisby, why would you want to keep the problems related to moving day from Timothy?

POSTREADING DISCUSSION: Students Skim Chapter; Discussion; Teacher Writes On Board

C In what ways has Mrs. Frisby shown her courage in this chapter?

CHAPTER 11 — In the Library; CHAPTER 12 — Isabella

VOCABULARY:

C

apparent	discern	irrelevantly	presumably	rarity
corridor	explicit	laboriously	pry	recessed
destination	freight	overwhelming	radiated	scuffle

PREREADING DISCUSSION:

Ev If you were Mrs. Frisby, what questions would you ask Mr. Ages and the rats? Read to find out how many of your questions are answered in the next two chapters and how many other questions are raised.

POSTREADING DISCUSSION: Teacher Writes On Board

Ev Which of your questions were answered and what new questions were raised?

JOURNAL WRITING: Teacher Reads; Students Write

Read the passage beginning, "Just as we reached the flood it happened," and ending with, "There was no other way to run; they had us encircled."

Sy Write a conversation that could have taken place among the men who were catching the rats.

MRS. FRISBY AND THE RATS OF NIMH

CHAPTER 13 — A Powder for Dragon; CHAPTER 14 — The Marketplace

VOCABULARY:

contrite	disinterested	encircled	intense	scrutiny
converged	drowsy	entangled	recount	upholstered
contrary	efficient	flail	research	vague
dependable	elegant	glumly	satchel	visible delight

PREREADING DISCUSSION:

Do you think the rats will help Mrs. Frisby? Read to find out if the rats help Mrs. Frisby and what other dangers Mrs. Frisby volunteers to do.

POSTREADING DISCUSSION: Teacher Writes On Board

In what ways will Mrs. Frisby be relieved to know the story of her husband's death? How will she be upset by the story? (List the responses.)

JOURNAL WRITING: Students Write

Ev

If you had seen the large mound of food in the marketplace, how would you have felt and what would you have done?

CHAPTER 15 — In the Cage; CHAPTER 16 — The Maze

VOCABULARY:

C

biologist	donned	inextricably	mercy	thrust
captivity	frenzy	injection	mutation	uncertainty
concealed	futile	illusion	neurologist	underestimating
device	incinerator	maze	partitions	

PREREADING DISCUSSION:

Ev

Why do you think the rats were caught? What clues does the chapter title "In the Cage" give you? Read to find out why the rats were captured.

POSTREADING DISCUSSION: Students Skim Chapters

In what different ways do you think a rat could escape from the laboratory?

MRS. FRISBY AND THE RATS OF NIMH

JOURNAL WRITING: Students Skim Chapters; Students Draw And Write

Ap/ Sy | Skim chapter 16. Draw the maze the rats had to run and label each section of it (where the electric shock and the trap were, etc.).

CHAPTER 17 — A Lesson in Reading; CHAPTER 18 — The Air Ducts

VOCABULARY:

C

complication	cubical	ducts	incurring	reluctant
comradeship	detect	formula	plaintive	submitted
consternation	distinguish	grid	predict	vent

PREREADING DISCUSSION: Teacher Writes On Board

An | What steps would you use to teach a rat to read? Why? Read to find out how the biologists teach the rats to read.

POSTREADING DISCUSSION: Teacher Writes On Board

Ev | How would these chapters be different if the rats had not learned to read? (Chain the responses in the space provided.)

JOURNAL WRITING: Students Write

Sy | Write about what you think would have happened if the rats had not learned to read.

CHAPTER 19 —The Boniface Estate; CHAPTER 20 — The Main Hall

VOCABULARY:

C

access	bungle	engrossed	puny	skeptical
artificial	chandelier	gestured	secure	suspicious
beckoned	debated	procession	silos	turf

MRS. FRISBY AND THE RATS OF NIMH

PREREADING DISCUSSION:

`Ev` How would being able to read benefit the rats when they were on their own?

POSTREADING DISCUSSION: Teacher Reads; Discussion

Read aloud the passage beginning, "All the time they stood there, the steady procession of rats continued," and ending with, "Why, live without stealing, of course. That's the whole idea. That's the plan."

`An` How would "life without stealing" be different from the way the rats had been living? (List the responses.)

JOURNAL WRITING: Students Write

`Ev` Is it right for the rats to take the things from Mr. Fitzgibbon to start their "life without stealing"? Why or why not?

CHAPTER 21 — The Toy Tinker; CHAPTER 22 — Thorn Valley

VOCABULARY:

`C`

acquaintance	descendents	habitation	permanently	scavengers
collapsed	drought	intentionally	pessimist	thrived
cynical	exterminate	irrigation	preferably	versatility

PREREADING DISCUSSION: Teacher Writes On Board

`Ev` Do you think the rats liked the big house in which they were staying on the Boniface Estate? Give reasons they might have liked and disliked it.

POSTREADING DISCUSSION: Teacher Writes On Board

`C` What do people mean when they say they're in a "rat race"?

`C` What do the rats mean when they say they're in a "people race"?

`An` What's good and bad about being in a rat/people race? (List the responses.)

MRS. FRISBY AND THE RATS OF NIMH

JOURNAL WRITING: Teacher Reads; Students Write

Read aloud the passage beginning, "Don't you see, Jenner, if we ever did anything like that, they'd figure out who we are and what we know?" and ending with, "We've already got a civilization."

Ev Design a rat-sized poster explaining the value of Jenner's point of view about the need to convince the rats to follow him.

CHAPTER 23 — Captured; CHAPTER 24 — Seven Dead Rats

VOCABULARY:

C
anticipated	cyanide	electrocuted	incinerated	solitude
associating	denounced	epidemic	inherited	transferred
colander	distressing	expectantly	secretive	urgent

PREREADING DISCUSSION:

Ev Do you think Mrs. Frisby will be successful in putting the medicine in Dragon's food? Why or why not?

An What other danger does she face on this mission? Read to find out how she fares.

POSTREADING DISCUSSION:

Ev How do you think Mrs. Frisby will be able to warn Nicodemus?

JOURNAL WRITING: Students Write

 Sy Write a note from Mrs. Frisby to Nicodemus warning him of the danger.

CHAPTER 25 — Escape; CHAPTER 26 — At the Meeting

VOCABULARY:

C
coincidence	defiant	hindmost	protested	semicircle
cryptically	deposited	impasse	pulley	suspicious
defective	exert	mechanized	scaffolding	vertical

MRS. FRISBY AND THE RATS OF NIMH

PREREADING DISCUSSION:

An How do you think Mrs. Frisby will be able to escape? How many different ways can you think of? (List the responses.)

POSTREADING DISCUSSION:

Ev What do you think would happen if some rats didn't stay behind to fool the exterminators?

JOURNAL WRITING: Students Write

Sy Write what you want to say to the rats from Mrs. Frisby's viewpoint.

CHAPTER 27 — The Doctor; CHAPTER 28 — Epilogue

VOCABULARY:

C
antidote	colony	furrow	inexorable	scurried
bramble	deliberation	futile	intertwining	tuft
calculated	dispatched	incredulously	revive	writhed

PREREADING DISCUSSION:

An What kinds of dangers will the rats who choose to stay behind face? Read to see what happens to them.

POSTREADING DISCUSSION:

Ev Do you think Mrs. Frisby and her children go to visit the rats?

Ev What do you think happens to Timothy and the other children during their lives?

JOURNAL WRITING: Students Write

Sy Imagine that Jeremy flies a note to Mrs. Frisby from the rats. What does the note say?

CULMINATING ACTIVITIES

POSTREADING DISCUSSION:

Ev Which was your favorite/least favorite character and why?

Ev What was your most favorite/least favorite part of the story and why?

Ev Would you recommend the book to others? Why or why not?

MRS. FRISBY AND THE RATS OF NIMH

STORY FRAME: Discussion; Students Read; Teacher Writes On Board; Students Fill In Story Frames

Have the students fill in the characters and setting on their story frames. Discuss the plot and then have the students review their chapter fill-in summaries. Ask the class to brainstorm major events in the story (list these on the board). Consolidate statements and ideas until everyone has an understanding of the summary. Then have the students fill in the summary sections of their story frames.

JOURNAL WRITING: Students Write

Have each student choose one of the following culminating activities:

• Explain a trip that Mrs. Frisby and her family make to visit the rats.

• Write a letter to the author describing your reaction to the book.

• What happened to the doctor? Did he stop his search for the rats? Why or why not?

• What happened to Jeremy?

• How do Mrs. Frisby's children turn out differently from the other mice? What do they do?

MRS. FRISBY AND THE RATS OF NIMH

MATH

MEASUREMENT/GRAPHING:

Have the students run a maze like the rats might have run in the story. Clock, record, and graph the results. Help the students draw conclusions from the graph.

SOCIAL STUDIES

CURRENT EVENTS:

Have the students study magazine/newspaper articles and TV/radio reports on animal rights issues.

DECISION-MAKING:

Ask the students to compare and contrast the rats' knowledge of right and wrong to that of ordinary rats.

SCIENCE

ANIMAL RIGHTS:

Have the class discuss or debate the issue of animal rights and scientific experimentation with animals as these topics relate to the rats in the book.

FINE ARTS

REPLICAS:

Have each student make a replica of the rats' tunnel, the owl's tree, Mrs. Frisby's home, or other locations described in the story.

COLLAGE:

Instruct each student to make a collage of shiny things Jeremy might have collected.

My Side Of The Mountain

MY SIDE OF THE MOUNTAIN

K 1. Who is the author of this book?_____

To whom is this book dedicated? _____

CHAPTER 1 — In Which I Hole Up in a Snowstorm

Rewrite sentences 2 - 4 on another piece of paper. Look up the underlined words in the dictionary.

C 2. She seemed restless and pulled at her <u>tethers</u>.

C 3. Water pours between the wet boulders and <u>cascades</u> into the valley below.

C 4. I tried to whistle but couldn't <u>purse</u> my shaking lips.

Ap 5. On another piece of paper, draw the interior of his tree cave and describe it.

Ev 6. What kind of food supplies might he have? _____

_____

Sy 7. Design another lamp he might use and describe it.

C 8. What did he mean by: "I think the storm is dying down because the tree is not crying so much"? _____

_____

An 9. Where do you think The Baron put the snow he dug?_____

_____

Ev 10. If you were facing your first snowstorm in a small tree cave, how would you feel?_____

_____

Sy 11. Make up your own recipe for acorn pancakes that is different from the one in the book. _____

_____

Sy 12. What different title would you give this chapter? Why? _____

_____

An 13. On another piece of paper, write a summary of the chapter.

MY SIDE OF THE MOUNTAIN
Individual Learning Unit Cont.

CHAPTER 2 — In Which I Get Started on This Venture

Rewrite sentences 14 - 16 on another piece of paper. Look up the underlined words in the dictionary.

C 14. The man in the store gave me some <u>tinder</u> to catch the sparks from the flint and steel.

C 15. It was a clear, <u>athletic</u> stream that rushed and splashed.

C 16. I cut off a green twig and began to <u>whittle</u>.

Ev 17. Have you ever thought about running away? Explain. _____

_____

_____

_____

_____

_____

_____

_____

_____

Ap 18. On another piece of paper, draw and label the things he left with.

Sy 19. On another piece of paper, sketch and describe another kind of shelter different from those in the book.

C 20. List the things that went wrong the first night. _____

_____

_____

_____

An 21. If you caught a fish with mosquitoes in its stomach, what would you use for bait? Why? _____

Sy 22. What different title would you give this chapter? Why? _____

_____

An 23. On another piece of paper, write a summary of the chapter.

MY SIDE OF THE MOUNTAIN

CHAPTER 3 — In Which I Find Gribley's Farm

Rewrite sentences 24 - 26 on another piece of paper. Look up the underlined words in the dictionary.

C   **24.** Roller-coasting up <u>ravines</u> and down hills was a mound of rocks.

C   **25.** If I didn't have to cut <u>boughs</u> for a bed I would have fish for dinner.

C   **26.** River birch has <u>combustible</u> oil in it.

Sy   **27.** Write a letter to the librarian as if you were Sam.

_____

_____

_____

_____

_____

_____

_____

_____

_____

_____

_____

_____

An   **28.** Where else could Sam have found an old map? _____

_____

Sy   **29.** What different title would you give this chapter? Why? _____

_____

An   **30.** On another piece of paper, write a summary of the chapter.

CHAPTER 4— In Which I Find Many Useful Plants

Rewrite sentences 31 - 33 on another piece of paper. Look up the underlined words in the dictionary.

C **31.** There was a slight <u>depression</u> where the basement had been.

C **32.** Too many leaves had turned to <u>loam</u>.

C **33.** I collected almost a <u>peck</u> of mussels.

C **34.** Why did Sam watch what the birds and animals ate?

_____

_____

_____

An **35.** What kinds of food does a stream have in it? _____

_____

_____

K **36.** List the eight different trees he found or saw.

_____

_____

_____

_____

Ap **37.** On another piece of paper, draw a map of what you think the farm might look like. Include the apple and walnut trees, the marsh, the ruined house, and the carved beech tree. Label them.

Sy **38.** What different title would you give this chapter? Why? _____

_____

_____

An **39.** On another piece of paper, write a summary of the chapter.

MY SIDE OF THE MOUNTAIN

CHAPTER 5 — About the Old Trees

Rewrite sentences 40 - 42 on another piece of paper. Look up the underlined words in the dictionary.

C   **40.** I could build a back <u>extension</u> around it.

C   **41.** Great-grandfather's farm was somewhat <u>remote</u>.

C   **42.** I discovered a <u>gorge</u> splashing down on black rocks.

Ap   **43.** On another piece of paper, draw what you think a Dogtooth Violet looks like and use the correct colors. Write a description of it.

K   **44.** What part of the Dogtooth Violet can be eaten? _____
_____

K   **45.** What did it taste like? _____
_____

C   **46.** Why did Sam wrap the crayfish in leaves and stuff them in his pocket?

_____

_____

_____

_____

_____

Sy   **47.** What different title would you give this chapter? Why? _____
_____

_____

An   **48.** On another piece of paper, write a summary of this chapter.

CHAPTER 6 — In Which I Meet One of My Own Kind and Have a Terrible Time Getting Away

Rewrite sentences 49 - 51 on another piece of paper. Look up the underlined words in the dictionary.

C **49.** She stood up and <u>escorted</u> me down the mountain.

C **50.** She <u>puckered</u> her forehead.

C **51.** My <u>snares</u> and traps were set.

C **52.** What three kinds of meat had Sam eaten?

_____

_____

_____

Sy **53.** Design a different snare you think would work. Explain how it operates.

_____

_____

_____

_____

Ev **54.** What would you have done with the old lady? _____

_____

An **55.** How do you think a duck hawk could hunt for a human? _____

_____

_____

_____

Sy **56.** What different title would you give this chapter? Why? _____

_____

An **57.** On another piece of paper, write a summary of this chapter.

CHAPTER 7 — The King's Provider

Rewrite sentences 58 - 60 on another piece of paper. Look up the underlined words in the dictionary.

C   **58.** I was shaking from <u>exertion</u>.

C   **59.** A snapping turtle would view a trout head with <u>relish</u>.

C   **60.** How was I going to climb the <u>sheer</u> wall?

K   **61.** Where do duck hawks nest?

_____

_____

K   **62.** What did Sam have for dinner?

_____

K   **63.** What did Sam have for breakfast?

_____

_____

C   **64.** What did Sam name his falcon and why? _____

_____

_____

Sy   **65.** What different name would you have given the falcon? Why? _____

_____

_____

Ap   **66.** Draw a picture of Frightful and describe it.

Sy   **67.** What different title would you give this chapter? Why? _____

_____

An   **68.** On another piece of paper, write a summary of this chapter.

MY SIDE OF THE MOUNTAIN
Individual Learning Unit Cont.

CHAPTER 8 — A Brief Account of What I Did About the First Man Who Was After Me

Rewrite sentences 69 - 70 on another piece of paper. Look up the underlined words in the dictionary.

C   **69.** I fed Frightful the more <u>savory</u> bites.

C   **70.** The Jack-in-the-Pulpits were <u>acrid</u>.

K   **71.** What were the "savory bites" Sam fed Frightful?

_____

_____

Ev   **72.** Why do you think Frightful liked those? _____

_____

_____

K   **73.** Doing what to a falcon makes it easier to train? _____

_____

_____

C   **74.** Why didn't Sam go to his tree? _____

_____

_____

C   **75.** Why was the fire marshal there? _____

_____

_____

Sy   **76.** What different title would you give this chapter? Why? _____

_____

_____

An   **77.** On another piece of paper, write a summary of the chapter.

© 1990 by Incentive Publications, Inc., Nashville, TN.

CHAPTER 9 — In Which I Learn To Season My Food

Rewrite sentences 78 - 80 on another piece of paper. Look up the underlined words in the dictionary.

C 78. The box trap had caught <u>numerous</u> rabbits.

C 79. He gave me a <u>lecture</u> I would never forget.

C 80. He vanished under a <u>scant</u> cover of bloodroot leaves.

K 81. Why does the sight of a closed trap excite Sam? _____

_____

Ev 82. Why do you think the weasel was not afraid of Sam and chattered at him so much? _____

_____

_____

Ev 83. Why do you think Sam called the weasel "The Baron"? _____

_____

_____

Sy 84. What different name would you give the weasel and why? _____

_____

_____

K 85. What two ways did Sam think of to get a deer? _____

_____

_____

K 86. What four different types of wood did he use in this chapter? _____

_____

_____

Sy 87. What different title would you give this chapter? Why? _____

_____

An 88. On another piece of paper, write a summary of the chapter.

CHAPTER 10 — How a Door Came To Me

Rewrite sentences 89 - 91 on another piece of paper. Look up the underlined words in the dictionary.

C 89. He was loping at my feet like a bouncing ball.

C 90. I tried to provoke him with a stick.

C 91. Leaves scuttled about.

K 92. What did Sam know was a good way to preserve food? _____

_____

_____

C 93. Why do you need to use hardwood to smoke fish? _____

_____

_____

Ap 94. On another piece of paper, draw three steps you think you should take to smoke a fish. Briefly describe each step.

C 95. What do you think he meant when he wrote, "I think I grew an inch on venison." _____

_____

_____

_____

Sy 96. What different title would you give this chapter? Why? _____

_____

_____

_____

An 97. On another piece of paper, write a summary of the chapter.

MY SIDE OF THE MOUNTAIN

CHAPTER 11 — In Which Frightful Learns Her ABC's

Rewrite sentences 98 - 99 on another piece of paper. Look up the underlined words in the dictionary.

C   **98.** What I needed was a <u>vessel</u> that was big enough.

C   **99.** My sweaters were <u>frayed</u>.

K   **100.** What is needed to tan hide? _____

_____

_____

C   **101.** What was Sam's problem with tanning the hide? _____

_____

_____

C   **102.** How did Sam solve his problem?_____

_____

_____

Ap   **103.** On another piece of paper, write the frog soup recipe like a real recipe. List all the ingredients and amounts first (you'll have to make up the amounts), then write the instructions.

C   **104.** What does Sam mean by "feather word"? _____

_____

Ap   **105.** On another piece of paper, draw what you think the turtle shell lamp looked like. Label the parts.

Ev   **106.** Why do you think Baron stayed around Sam? _____

_____

K   **107.** What two kinds of flour did he make?_____

_____

Sy   **108.** What different title would you give this chapter. Why? _____

_____

An   **109.** On another piece of paper, write a summary of the chapter.

CHAPTER 12 — In Which I Find a Real Live Man

Rewrite sentences 110 - 112 on another piece of paper. Look up the underlined words in the dictionary.

C   **110.** It started me into the day with a <u>vengeance</u>.

C   **111.** While I bathed, Frightful <u>preened</u> herself.

C   **112.** Baron Weasel would glance <u>furtively</u> at us.

Ap   **113.** Rewrite the mussel recipe. List all the ingredients and amounts first (you'll have to make up the amounts), then write the instructions.

_____

_____

_____

_____

_____

_____

_____

_____

_____

_____

Ev   **114.** Why do you think Sam called the man Bando? _____

_____

_____

An   **115.** List three things Bando did that Sam hadn't done before. _____

_____

_____

Sy   **116.** What different title would you give this chapter? Why? _____

_____

An   **117.** On another piece of paper, write a summary of the chapter.

MY SIDE OF THE MOUNTAIN
Individual Learning Unit Cont.

CHAPTER 13— In Which the Autumn Provides Food and Loneliness

Rewrite sentences 118 - 120 on another piece of paper. Look up the underlined words in the dictionary.

C   **118.** September <u>blazed</u> a trail into the mountains.

C   **119.** Baron Weasel might be changing his summer fur for his white winter <u>mantle</u>.

C   **120.** I was lonely and on the <u>verge</u> of tears.

C   **121.** Why was Sam so lonely? _____

_____

_____

_____

Ap   **122.** On another piece of paper, draw what you think the clay fireplace looked like. Describe it.

C   **123.** After the fireplace was built and operating, what was Sam's problem? ____

_____

_____

C   **124.** How did Sam solve the problem? _____

_____

_____

C   **125.** How was Frightful helpful in finding the problem? _____

_____

_____

_____

Sy   **126.** What different title would you give this chapter? Why? _____

_____

_____

An   **127.** On another piece of paper, write a summary of the chapter.

© 1990 by Incentive Publications, Inc., Nashville, TN.

CHAPTER 14 — In Which We All Learn About Halloween

Rewrite sentences 128 - 130 on another piece of paper. Look up the underlined words in the dictionary.

C **128.** It was a good <u>scheme</u>.

C **129.** The Baron came <u>sprinting</u> into sight.

C **130.** I was <u>dismayed</u> to see the mess in my house.

K **131.** What things did Sam have to race the squirrels for? _____

_____

_____

K **132.** List the animals that ate and shared in Sam's "party." _____

_____

_____

Sy **133.** What was a different menu you think Sam could have had for the party? ___

_____

_____

_____

C **134.** What problems did Sam have after the party? _____

_____

_____

C **135.** How did he solve the problem? _____

_____

_____

C **136.** What does it mean, "To animals might is right"? _____

_____

Sy **137.** What different title would you give this chapter? Why? _____

_____

An **138.** On another piece of paper, write a summary of the chapter.

CHAPTER 15 — In Which I Find Out What to Do With Hunters

Rewrite sentences 139 - 141 on another piece of paper. Look up the underlined words in the dictionary.

C   **139.** They would be on every hill and <u>dale</u>.

C   **140.** Frightful <u>rustled</u> her wings.

C   **141.** When <u>embers</u> were glowing, I had a good dinner.

K   **142.** Write at least two things Sam did the first day of hunting season. _____

_____

_____

K   **143.** What did he do the second day of hunting season? _____

_____

_____

C   **144.** What does this mean:"I stuffed myself until I felt kindly toward all men"? ____

_____

_____

Ev   **145.** How would you feel and what would you do if you were Sam during the hunting season? _____

_____

_____

Sy   **146.** On another piece of paper, draw three things you would make from the deerhide if you were Sam. Describe them.

Sy   **147.** What different title would you give this chapter? Why? _____

_____

An   **148.** On another piece of paper, write a summary of the chapter.

CHAPTER 16 — In Which Trouble Begins

Rewrite sentences 149 - 151 on another piece of paper. Look up the underlined words in the dictionary.

C   **149.** Those beautiful marks gave her much of her <u>superb</u> <u>dignity</u>.

C   **150.** Her <u>plumage</u> had changed during autumn.

C.   **151.** I walked to the main <u>intersection</u> of town.

Ap   **152.** On another piece of paper, draw a picture of Sam's deerskin suit.

Describe it.

Ev   **153.** Why do you think Sam went to town? _____

_____

_____

An   **154.** Sam tells the new boy that he's doing research at the Gribley farm. What kind of research is Sam doing? _____

_____

_____

K   **155.** List the seven birds mentioned in this chapter. _____

_____

_____

C   **156.** Why would Sam need a big woodpile for the winter? _____

_____

Ev   **157.** Do you think Mr. Jacket will come to visit Sam? Why or why not? _____

_____

_____

Sy   **158.** What different title would you give this chapter? Why? _____

_____

An   **159.** On another piece of paper, write a summary of the chapter.

CHAPTER 17 — In Which I Pile Up Wood and Go On With Winter

Rewrite sentences 160 - 162 on another piece of paper. Look up the underlined words in the dictionary.

C **160.** Frightful and I would <u>reel</u> down the hill.

C **161.** On the ground Frightful would cover her <u>quarry</u>.

C **162.** With the food as a <u>bracer</u> for the day, Frightful and I would set out.

Ap **163.** Draw a picture of the many woodpiles he made. Describe it.

K **164.** List three kinds of game Frightful would catch. _____

_____

_____

Ev **165.** What do you think made the winter nights so special for Sam? _____

_____

Sy **166.** What different title would you give this chapter? Why? _____

_____

An **167.** On another piece of paper, write a summary of the chapter.

CHAPTER 18 — In Which I Learn About Birds and People

Rewrite sentences 168 - 170 on another piece of paper. Look up the underlined words in the dictionary.

C **168.** Frightful and I ate the mountain <u>harvest</u>.

C **169.** I had read about loneliness during the <u>bleakness</u> of winter.

C **170.** I checked my <u>cache</u> of wild onions.

C **171.** How did Sam think winter was more exciting than summer? _____

_____

K **172.** List the three newspaper articles about the boy living in the mountains.

_____

_____

_____

Ap **173.** On another piece of paper, write your own newspaper article about the wild boy of the Catskills. Give it an original title.

C **174.** List the dinner menu.

_____

_____

_____

An **175.** List a different menu Sam could have had.

_____

_____

_____

Sy **176.** On another piece of paper, draw a different present you would have made for Bando if you were Sam. Describe it and what it's made of.

Sy **177.** What different title would you give this chapter? Why? _____

_____

An **178.** On another piece of paper, write a summary of the chapter.

CHAPTER 19 — In Which I Have a Good Look at Winter and Find Spring In the Snow

Rewrite sentences 179 - 181 on another piece of paper. Look up the underlined words in the dictionary.

C 179. I wandered the snowy <u>crags</u>.

C 180. I didn't have a moment of <u>fatigue</u>.

C 181. I had an <u>urgent</u> desire to return to my tree.

Ap 182. When you don't have TV, radio, or newspapers, how do you know what the weather will be? _____

_____

_____

C 183. What did it mean, "I was really into the teeth of winter"? _____

_____

Ap 184. On another piece of paper, draw a picture of Sam's deer mouse visitor. (Look it up in the encyclopedia.) Describe it.

C 185. Why was Sam excited about the great horned owl? _____

_____

K 186. What does Baron Weasel eat?_____

_____

C 187. Explain,"January was a fierce month." _____

_____

K 188. After feeling aches and having a nosebleed, what did Sam eat? _____

_____

C 189. What was the problem with Sam's winter diet? _____

_____

Sy 190. What different title would you give this chapter? Why? _____

_____

An 191. On another piece of paper, write a summary of the chapter.

MY SIDE OF THE MOUNTAIN

Individual Learning Unit Cont.

CHAPTER 20 — More About the Spring in the Winter and the Beginning of My Story's End

Rewrite sentences 192 - 194 on another piece of paper. Look up the underlined words in the dictionary.

C   **192.** The activity gathered <u>momentum</u>.

C   **193.** I walked into the valley to scout for <u>edible</u> plants.

C   **194.** Frightful <u>hovered</u> above my head.

C   **195.** What did it mean, "The owl had broken the spell of winter"? _____

_____

_____

K   **196.** How many cups of maple sap does it take to make one cup of syrup? _____

An   **197.** How do you think the skunk cabbage got its name? _____

_____

_____

Ev   **198.** If you were Matt, would you write the true story of the wild boy or the made-up story? Why? _____

_____

Ev   **199.** Do you agree with Frightful: "You really want to be found or you would not have told Matt all you did"? Why? _____

_____

Sy   **200.** What different title would you give this chapter. Why? _____

_____

An   **201.** On another piece of paper, write a summary of the chapter.

© 1990 by Incentive Publications, Inc., Nashville, TN.

149

CHAPTER 21 — In Which I Cooperate With the Ending

Rewrite sentences 202 - 204 on another piece of paper. Look up the underlined words in the dictionary.

C   **202.** The <u>circumstances</u> that brought us all together were no more.

C   **203.** I had not counted <u>notches</u> in weeks.

C   **204.** I lit the <u>tallow</u> candle.

Sy   **205.** Make up a four line verse to the "cold water song."

_____

_____

_____

_____

K   **206.** Why did Sam blindfold Matt? _____

_____

_____

Ap   **207.** On another piece of paper, draw a picture of what you think Matt's hat looked like. Describe it.

K   **208.** List the ingredients that went into snapping turtle soup. _____

_____

_____

K   **209.** List all the people that visited Sam in this chapter. _____

_____

_____

_____

Sy   **210.** What different title would you give this chapter? Why? _____

_____

_____

An   **211.** On another piece of paper, write a summary of this chapter.

CHAPTER 22 — In Which the City Comes to Me

Rewrite sentences 212 - 214 on another piece of paper. Look up the underlined words in the dictionary.

C 212. <u>Hordes</u> were coming.

C 213. I rode downhill on an aspen <u>sapling</u>.

C 214. Your mother said she was going to give you a <u>decent</u> home.

C 215. What did it mean: "June burst over the mountains"?_____

_____

_____

Ev 216. How would you feel if you were Sam and the photographer took a picture of you? _____

_____

C 217. What was Sam's mother's problem with the newspaper stories? _____

_____

C 218. How did she solve it? _____

_____

_____

Ev 219. On another piece of paper, draw what you think the finished house would look like. Describe it.

Ev 220. Where do you think Baron Weasel went?_____

_____

Ev 221. Did you like the ending of the book? Why or why not? _____

_____

Sy 222. On another piece of paper, write another ending for the book.

MY SIDE OF THE MOUNTAIN

1. Sew some mittens out of leather or leather-like material.

2. Write a book of recipes Sam may have used.

3. Pretend you are Sam and write a diary of what you did and felt for a week.

4. Draw, color, and describe at least six plants and animals Sam encountered.

5. Make a diorama of a part of the story.

6. Build two different snares Sam may have used.

7. Draw a detailed map of a park or some woods near you. Color it and include a key.

8. Cook one of the recipes in the book (you might have to substitute other ingredients) and share it with your class or reading group.

MY SIDE OF THE MOUNTAIN

PRELIMINARY ACTIVITIES

GETTING READY TO READ:

K | Who is the author? *Jean Craighead George*

K | Has the book won any awards? *Newbery Medal, ALA Notable Book, and Hans Christian Anderson International Award*

Ap | What other books has Jean Craighead George written? *Julie of the Wolves, The Cry of the Crow, Summer of the Falcon*

Ap | Where do you think the story takes place? *answers will vary*

Ap | How many characters might the story have? *answers will vary*

An | What do you think the story is about? *answers will vary*

PREREADING DISCUSSION:

An | How would living in the mountain be different from living in a city? (List student responses on the board.)

JOURNAL WRITING: Discussion; Students Write

Ev | What would you miss most about the city if you lived in the mountains? Why? And what would you miss about the mountains if you lived in the city? Why?

CHAPTER 1 — Hole Up in a Snowstorm; CHAPTER 2 — I Get Started ...

VOCABULARY:

C | tethers   whittle   cascade   purse   tinder   athletic

PREREADING DISCUSSION:

Ev | Have you ever wanted to run away? What reasons did you have? Sam has run away in these chapters. See what his reasons were.

POSTREADING DISCUSSION: Teacher Writes on Board

C | Skim the chapters to see what articles and skills Sam needed to get started surviving in the woods.?

JOURNAL WRITING: Students Write

Ev | What things would you have brought with you if you were Sam? Why?

MY SIDE OF THE MOUNTAIN

CHAPTER 3 — I Find Gribley's Farm; CHAPTER 4 — I Find Useful Plants

VOCABULARY:

C	ravine	browse	acreage	combustible	independent
	depression	migration	edible	peck	

PREREADING DISCUSSION: Teacher Writes on Board

An | How many ways is a fire useful in the woods? (List student responses.) See how fire is useful to Sam in this chapter.

POSTREADING DISCUSSION:

Ev | What do you think Sam's idea is? Discuss your theories.

JOURNAL WRITING: Teacher Reads; Students Draw

Read aloud the passage beginning, "At high noon I stepped onto a mountain meadow," and ending with, "They looked like pebbles beneath those trees."

Ev | Have the students draw the scene.

CHAPTER 5 — The Old, Old Tree; CHAPTER 6 — I Meet One of My Own Kind

VOCABULARY:

C	extension	snare	vague	remote	obvious
	noose	gorge	cavity	inspiration	escorted
	primitive	wiry	puckered	dandelions	teetered

PREREADING DISCUSSION:

An | How many different ways can you hollow out a tree? See how Sam goes about hollowing out a tree and beginning to think more like a mountain boy than a city boy.

POSTREADING DISCUSSION: Students Skim; Teacher Writes On Board

C | Skim these two chapters for all the different foods Sam found and ate. (Write the students' responses on the board.)

JOURNAL WRITING: Students Write

Ev | How would you have dealt with the little old lady who asked Sam to help her pick strawberries? Was Sam right to have done what he did? Why or why not?

MY SIDE OF THE MOUNTAIN

CHAPTER 7 — The King's Provider; CHAPTER 8 — A Brief Account...

VOCABULARY:

exertion	falcon	tuber	relish	depart
sheer	minnow	savory	sprint	acrid

PREREADING DISCUSSION:

 How do you think Sam will go about catching a falcon, a bird of prey, alive? What problems might he encounter?

POSTREADING DISCUSSION: Teacher Writes On Board

 What do you think would have happened to Sam had the fire warden caught him?

JOURNAL WRITING: Students Write

 Write a dialogue which Sam and the fire warden might have had if they had met. (Remember to use quotation marks correctly.)

CHAPTER 9 — I Learn to Season My Food; CHAPTER 10 — How a Door Came to Me

VOCABULARY:

numerous	provoke	misshapen	device
scant	scuttled	residue	rumpus
preserve	berate	venison	lecture

PREREADING DISCUSSION:

 What seasonings do you use on your food? What would things taste like without any seasonings? Which seasoning do you think is most important? Sam makes a seasoning in these chapters. Read to find out what it is.

POSTREADING DISCUSSION:

 What do you think the title of this chapter meant? Why?

JOURNAL WRITING: Students Write

Read aloud the passage beginning, "Bushes cracked, leaves scuttled, and a man with a rifle came into the meadow," and ending with, "I stayed on the bed all morning, telling the fierce little bundle of feathers in my hand that there was deer meat in store for her if she would just wait with me."

Have the students write about how they felt as the poacher came closer to Sam.

MY SIDE OF THE MOUNTAIN

CHAPTER 11 — Frightful Learns Her ABC's; CHAPTER 12 — I Find a Real Live Man

VOCABULARY:

C

vessel	glance	furtively	frayed
talons	preened	racketeer	

PREREADING DISCUSSION:

Ev What kinds of things do you think Sam will make out of the deer hide? Why? Read to find out what he does with it.

POSTREADING DISCUSSION: Teacher Writes on Board

An How was Bando different from all the other people Sam has seen or come into contact with in the woods? (List students' responses.)

JOURNAL WRITING: Students Write

An Write a letter to Bando from Sam explaining your feelings or write a letter to Sam from Bando explaining how you felt about the time you had together.

CHAPTER 13 — Autumn Provides Food; CHAPTER 14 — We All Learn...

VOCABULARY:

C

scheme	verge	mallet	tether	cavort
sprint	abandon	revive	bashful	dismay
sensation	ventilate	indignity	blazed (trail)	lure
molar	migration	ferocity	mantle (weasel's)	

PREREADING DISCUSSION:

An What are the signs of autumn in your town? What happens to the plants and animals? What's the weather like? Find out what signs of autumn Sam sees in the woods and how he prepares for the coming winter.

POSTREADING DISCUSSION: Teacher Writes on Board

Ev How could Sam have made Halloween a better experience? What do you think he has learned from this experience? (List students' responses.)

JOURNAL WRITING: Teacher Reads; Students Write

Sy Read to the students the passage beginning, "I lit the fire, closed the flap of the door and listened to the wind bring the first frost to the mountain." Have the students write their own versions of Sam's close brush with death.

MY SIDE OF THE MOUNTAIN

CHAPTER 15 — I Find Out What To Do With Hunters; CHAPTER 16 — Trouble Begins

VOCABULARY:

intersection	dole	stupidity	rustled	moral
research	embers	plumage	superb	cosmetic

PREREADING DISCUSSION: Teacher Writes on Board

An Why do you think Sam might find hunters frightening? In what way might he also find them useful? (List students' responses.)

POSTREADING DISCUSSION:

Ev What would have happened had Sam not remembered to stockpile wood for the winter?

JOURNAL WRITING: Students Write

Sy Write about the "Daniel Boone" boy you met in the drugstore from the "Mr. Jacket" boy's point of view.

CHAPTER 17 — I Pile Up Wood; CHAPTER 18 — I Learn About Birds and People

VOCABULARY:

C

reel	bleak	absorbent	conservationists	serenade
sanguine	quarry	ingenious	temptation	edition
cache	bracer	reluctant	sensationalism	
harvest	portico	insulate	originated	

PREREADING DISCUSSION:

Ap Describe a cozy winter evening in your house. Sam experiences happy winter evenings in these chapters.

POSTREADING DISCUSSION: Teacher Writes on Board

Ev List all the adjectives you can think of to describe Sam's father's reaction to his son's accomplishment.

JOURNAL WRITING: Students Skim Chapters and Write

Sy Skim the chapters for the specifics of the newspaper articles written about the wild boy of the Catskills. Write your own article explaining the truth.

MY SIDE OF THE MOUNTAIN

CHAPTER 19 — I Have a Good Look at Winter; CHAPTER 20 — More About the Spring

VOCABULARY:

crag	hovered	swivel	weatherproof
fatigue	humanity	concoction	instincts
urgent	avalanche	treacherous	circulatory
momentum	barometer	resilient	forum

PREREADING DISCUSSION:

What are the signs of spring in your area? Read to find out how Sam tells that spring has come to the Catskills.

POSTREADING DISCUSSION:

Do you agree with Frightful's observation (in Sam's imaginary conversation) that Sam really wanted to be found or he wouldn't have told Matt as much as he did? Why or why not?

JOURNAL WRITING: Students Write

Do you think Matt will keep his bargain not to publish his article about Sam? Why or why not?

CHAPTER 21 — I Cooperate With the Ending; CHAPTER 22 — The City Comes to Me

VOCABULARY:

circumstances	decent	self-sufficient	notches
abundant	infer	editorials	tallow
portable	hordes	pondered	sapling

PREREADING DISCUSSION: Teacher Writes on Board

List in two columns on the board ways in which winter differs from spring. Consider food supply, friends, energy, etc. See how Sam's spring differs greatly from his wintertime friends and activities.

POSTREADING DISCUSSION: Teacher Writes on Board

From Sam's point of view, what were the advantages of living in the mountains and the advantages of being with people? List these on the board.

MY SIDE OF THE MOUNTAIN

JOURNAL WRITING: Teacher Reads; Students Write

Ev | Read to the students the passage beginning, "I was stunned. I was beginning to realize that this was not an overnight camping trip. . ." Have the students write how they would react to Sam's mother's statement and explain why.

CULMINATING ACTIVITIES

POSTREADING DISCUSSION:

Ev | How are you like Sam?

Ev | Would you want Sam for a friend? Why or why not?

Ev | What was your favorite part of the story? What was your least favorite?

STORY FRAME: Discussion; Students Read; Teacher Writes On Board; Students Fill In Story Frames

 | Have the students fill in the characters and setting on their story frames. Discuss the plot and then have the students review their chapter fill-in summaries. Ask the class to brainstorm major events in the story (list these on the board). Consolidate statements and ideas until everyone has an understanding of the summary. Then have the students fill in the summary sections of their story frames.

JOURNAL WRITING: Students Write

Ev | Students choose one of the following to do as a culminating activity:

- Write a last diary entry for Sam after his parents came.

- Write a letter to the author about your reaction to the book and questions you want to ask.

- Describe how the family got along after they moved to the mountains.

- Write a final newspaper story about the family.

MY SIDE OF THE MOUNTAIN

MATH

COOKING/MEASURING:

Make a recipe book and cook some of the foods Sam mentions in the story.

SOCIAL STUDIES

ANIMALS OF THE CATSKILLS:

Study the life cycles, food chains, and habits of the animals mentioned in the book.

SCIENCE

MAP:

Make a map of the Gribley farm. Include a key or legend to indicate trees, water, shelter, etc.

TIME LINE:

Construct a time line of the events in the story.

FINE ARTS

MODELS:

Construct models of the things Sam used in the book.

BRIDGE TO TERABITHIA

Individual Learning Unit

CHAPTER 1

C   **1.** Where does this chapter take place? _____

_____

Ap   **2.** Jess found if he tiptoed out of the house no one would hear him. What have you learned to do without making noise? _____

_____

Ap   **3.** Draw Miss Bessie with, "her big, brown droopy eyes" on another piece of paper.

Ap   **4.** Practice being like Brenda who, "pinched her nose with her pinky crooked delicately."

K   **5.** What chores did Jess have to do? _____

_____

Ap   **6.** What chores do you have to do around the house? _____

_____

C   **7.** On another piece of paper, describe these characters: Jess, May Belle, Joyce Ann, Miss Bessie, Ellie, Brenda, Mom, and Dad.

An   **8.** Which character is least like you? Why? _____

_____

_____

An   **9.** Which character in this chapter is the most like you? Why? _____

_____

_____

Ev   **10.** Why do you think the chapter was called, "Jesse Oliver Aarons, Jr."? _____

_____

_____

Sy   **11.** What other title would you give this chapter? Why? _____

_____

An   **12.** On another piece of paper, list the three main events of this chapter.

© 1990 by Incentive Publications, Inc., Nashville, TN.

CHAPTER 2

C   **13.** What did Jess make for the little girls for dinner? _____

_____

Ap   **14.** What would you have made for dinner? Why? _____

_____

_____

_____

Ap   **15.** On another piece of paper, draw the scene Jess drew in this chapter and describe it.

An   **16.** What things happen to show that Jess is lonely? _____

_____

_____

C   **17.** What do you think Jess's mother meant when she said Miss Edwards, "sounds like some kind of hippie"? _____

_____

_____

Ap   **18.** What would you have said to Jess the first time you saw him? Why? _____

_____

_____

Ev   **19.** Why do you think the chapter was called, "Leslie Burke"? _____

_____

_____

Sy   **20.** What other title would you give this chapter? Why? _____

_____

_____

An   **21.** On another piece of paper, list the three main events of this chapter.

CHAPTER 3

On another sheet of paper, rewrite sentences 22 - 23 in your own words.

C   **22.** "Surprise swooshed up from the class like steam from a released radiator cap."

C   **23.** "It was as though he had swallowed grasshoppers."

An   **24.** On another piece of paper, compare the way Leslie and Jess dressed.

Ap   **25.** On another piece of paper, draw Mrs. Myers famous "first-day-of-school smile." Then practice doing it yourself.

K   **26.** What names did Jess think of for his book of drawings? _____

_____

_____

Ev   **27.** What names can you think of for Jess's book? _____

_____

_____

C   **28.** Why did Jess ask Leslie to run? _____

_____

Ev   **29.** Why do you think Jess didn't want to sit next to Leslie on the bus? _____

_____

_____

Ev   **30.** Why do you think the chapter was called, "The Fastest Kid in Fifth Grade"?

_____

_____

Sy   **31.** What other title would you give this chapter? Why? _____

_____

_____

An   **32.** On another piece of paper, list the three main events of this chapter.

CHAPTER 4

On another piece of paper, explain the meaning of sentences 33 - 34.

C   **33.** "Running wasn't fun anymore. And it was all Leslie's fault."

C   **34.** What did Jess mean when he felt, "It was the beginning of a new season in his life"?

C   **35.** What did Leslie mean when she said her parents were, "too hooked on money and success"? _____

_____

_____

An   **36.** How is Leslie different from you? _____

_____

_____

Ev   **37.** Do you think Jess is afraid of water? Why or why not?_____

_____

_____

Sy   **38.** On another piece of paper, write a paragraph describing your favorite hobby.

C   **39.** On another piece of paper, draw a picture of Janice Avery from her description in the book.

Sy   **40.** On another piece of paper, draw a picture of the imaginary castle of Terabithia.

Ev   **41.** Why do you think the chapter was called, "Rulers of Terabithia"? _____

_____

_____

Sy   **42.** What other title would you give this chapter? Why? _____

_____

_____

An   **43.** On another piece of paper, list the three main events of this chapter.

CHAPTER 5

C 44. What does it mean that Jess and Leslie both knew, "...that the real giant in their lives was Janice Avery"? _____

_____

C 45. What does it mean, "May Belle didn't want comfort, she wanted revenge."

_____

_____

Ev 46. How do Jess and Leslie feel about May Belle? How can you tell? _____

_____

_____

K 47. On another piece of paper, copy the note Leslie dictated and Jess wrote.

Ap 48. Practice reading the note in the "moony" voice Leslie spoke in.

Ev 49. What do you think would have happened if Janice Avery had not taken May Belle's Twinkies™? Why? _____

_____

_____

Ev 50. Why do you think the chapter was called, "The Giant Killers"? _____

_____

_____

_____

Sy 51. What other title would you give this chapter? Why? _____

_____

_____

An 52. On another piece of paper, list the three main events of this chapter.

CHAPTER 6

Ap   **53.** "Brenda screwed her face up in that ugly way she did." Practice doing this.

Ap   **54.** Describe the way your family or your friends look when they watch TV. _____

_____

_____

_____

An   **55.** How are Brenda and Ellie like Cinderella's step-sisters? _____

_____

_____

_____

An   **56.** On another piece of paper, compare the way Jess acts toward his younger and his older sisters.

Ev   **57.** How does Leslie's present to Jess show what good friends they are? _____

_____

_____

Ap   **58.** List the feelings Christmas brings to you.

_____

_____

_____

Ev   **59.** Why do you think the chapter was called, "The Coming of Prince Terrien"?

_____

_____

_____

Sy   **60.** What other title would you give this chapter? Why? _____

_____

_____

An   **61.** On another piece of paper, list the three main events of this chapter.

BRIDGE TO TERABITHIA — Individual Learning Unit Cont.

C   **62.** What does it mean, "Mr. Burke was inclined to be absentminded"? _____

_____

C   **63.** What did it mean that Terabithia needed, "...Leslie to make the magic"? _____

_____

_____

Ev   **64.** How do you think Leslie would feel if she went to Terabithia alone? Why? _____

_____

_____

An   **65.** How are Leslie's parents the same as and different from Jess's parents? _____

_____

_____

_____

C   **66.** When Leslie told Jess he could help her and her dad fix up their house, the author writes, "It was like all the lights coming back on after an electrical storm." What did it mean? _____

_____

_____

C   **67.** How does Jess feel when Leslie spends time with her dad? After Leslie tells Jess he can help? When he learns Janice Avery was crying? When May Belle follows him to Terabithia? Write your answers on a separate sheet of paper.

Ev   **68.** Can you understand his feelings in these situations? Why or why not? _____

_____

_____

Ev   **69.** Why do you think the chapter was called, "The Golden Room"? _____

_____

Sy   **70.** What other title would you give this chapter? Why? _____

_____

An   **71.** On another piece of paper, list the three main events of this chapter.

CHAPTER 8

Ev **72.** Why do you think Momma got mad at the preacher three years ago?

_____

_____

C **73.** What had happened to Jess's dad?_____

_____

_____

C **74.** What did Momma mean when she said, "We got a lot more than Easter clothes to worry about"?_____

_____

_____

Ev **75.** What kinds of things would you worry about if you were Jess's momma?

_____

_____

_____

Ap **76.** What kinds of things do you worry about now?_____

_____

_____

_____

Ap **77.** On another piece of paper, draw how Leslie looked when she went to church.

Ev **78.** Why do you think the chapter was called "Easter"? _____

_____

_____

Sy **79.** What other title would you give this chapter? Why? _____

_____

_____

An **80.** On another piece of paper, list the three main events of this chapter.

CHAPTER 9

C   **81.** On another piece of paper, copy sentences from the book that show the bad feelings Jess was having.

Ev   **82.** What would you do if you were Jess and had these feelings? _____

_____

_____

_____

_____

An   **83.** How would this chapter be different if it hadn't rained? _____

_____

_____

_____

An   **84.** How is the grove of pine trees like a church? _____

_____

_____

_____

Ev   **85.** Why do you think the chapter was called, "The Evil Spell"? _____

_____

_____

_____

Sy   **86.** What other title would you give this chapter? Why? _____

_____

_____

An   **87.** On another piece of paper, list the three main events of this chapter.

CHAPTER 10

Ev **88.** What kinds of jobs do you think Jess's dad could do and could not do? Explain your answer on another sheet of paper.

Sy **89.** Make up a dialogue between Jess and Leslie where Jess tells her how he feels about going to Terabithia. _____

_____

_____

An **90.** How do you think entering the art gallery was like stepping inside the pine grove? _____

_____

_____

Ap **91.** Draw the scene of the buffalo hunt that Jess saw.

Ev **92.** How was it a perfect day for Jess's parents? _____

_____

_____

An **93.** Why do you think the chapter was called "The Perfect Day"? _____

_____

_____

Sy **94.** What other title would you give this chapter? Why? _____

_____

_____

An **95.** List the three main events of this chapter. _____

_____

_____

_____

_____

CHAPTER 11

An 96. What did Jess do in the chapter to show that he didn't believe Leslie was dead? That he was angry? That he was sad? Write a paragraph explaining your answers.

Ev 97. If you were Jess, would you be able to eat all those pancakes? Why or why not? _____

_____

An 98. How were Jess's feelings like the scene of the buffalo hunt?_____

_____

_____

Ev 99. Do you think Leslie would have gone with Jess to Washington if he had asked for her? Write a paragraph explaining why or why not.

Ev 100. What do you want to do to Jess's older sisters when they pester him at breakfast? Why? _____

_____

_____

C 101. What does it mean to "pay your respects"? _____

_____

_____

Ev 102. Why do you think the chapter was called "No!"? _____

_____

_____

Sy 103. What other title would you give this chapter? Why? _____

_____

_____

An 104. List the three main events of this chapter. _____

_____

_____

_____

© 1990 by Incentive Publications, Inc., Nashville, TN.

CHAPTER 12

Ev 105. Why do you think Jess hit May Belle? _____
_____
_____

C 106. What did he do after he hit May Belle? _____
_____
_____

Ev 107. What do you think Jess really meant when he said, "I hate her. I wish I'd never seen her in my whole life"? _____
_____
_____

An 108. How are Jess's parents acting differently than they did earlier in the book?
_____
_____

Ev 109. In chapter two the author writes, "It made Jess ache inside to watch his dad grab the little ones to his shoulders, or lean down and hug them. It seemed to him that he had been thought too big for that since the day he was born." Did Jess get the love from his father that he always wanted in this chapter? Write a paragraph explaining your answer.

Ev 110. Why do you think the chapter was called "Stranded"? _____
_____
_____

Sy 111. What other title would you give this chapter? Why? _____
_____
_____

An 112. List the three main events of this chapter. _____
_____
_____
_____

CHAPTER 13

C   **113.** Draw a picture of the funeral wreath Jess made for Leslie.

Ev   **114.** What does it mean to have "magic in you"? _____

_____

_____

An   **115.** At one point in the book, Jess didn't want to go to Terabithia alone because there was no magic there without Leslie. How has that changed?

_____

_____

_____

Ap   **116.** How do you have magic in you? _____

_____

_____

Ev   **117.** Why do you think the chapter was called "Building the Bridge"? _____

_____

_____

Sy   **118.** What other title would you give this chapter? Why? _____

_____

_____

An   **119.** List the three main events of this chapter. _____

_____

BRIDGE TO TERABITHIA

1. Dress and act like one of the characters. Tell what happened to you in the book and how you felt about it.

2. Make your own pictures of parts of the book and explain them.

3. Keep a diary of one of the characters.

4. Create a model of your own secret place and explain it.

5. Design a detailed map of the area Jess and Leslie lived in. Label everything, including Terabithia.

6. Tape-record a story about the king and queen of Terabithia.

7. Give a speech explaining what you think happened to each of the other characters in the book, i.e., Miss Edmunds, Janice, Ellie, Brenda, etc.

8. Pretend you are Jess and make up a book of pictures.

9. Cook one of the recipes in the book (you might have to substitute other ingredients) and share it with your class or reading group.

BRIDGE TO TERABITHIA

PRELIMINARY ACTIVITIES

GETTING READY TO READ:

K Who is the author? *Katherine Paterson*

K Has the book won any awards? *Newbery Medal*

Ap What other books has Katherine Paterson written? *The Sign of the Chrysanthemum, Of Nightengales That Weep, The Master Puppeteer, The Great Gilly Hopkins, Angels and Other Strangers, Jacob Have I Loved*

K Who illustrated the book: *Donna Diamond*

K To whom is the book dedicated: *David Paterson and Lisa Hill*

Ap Where do you think the story takes place? *answers will vary*

Ap Who are the main characters? *answers will vary*

An What do you think the story is about? *answers will vary*

PREREADING DISCUSSION:

An Have you ever had a special place before?

Ap What kinds of things did you do there?

Ap How did you feel when you were there?

JOURNAL WRITING: Students Write

Ap Take yourself on a trip to your special place. Think about how you feel and what you would do if you were happy there or sad there. List what you would do in those times.

BRIDGE TO TERBITHIA

CHAPTER 1

VOCABULARY:

C	trot	grit	puny	whine	jab
	scrap	athletic	crud	obediently	discard
	cuds	trolled	scald	concert	prim

PREREADING DISCUSSION: Teacher Writes on Board

An In this chapter you will meet Jess's family. What questions do you have about them? (List all questions on the board.) Let's see how many of the questions are answered in this chapter.

POSTREADING DISCUSSION:

C What questions about Jess's family were answered? What new things did you learn?

C Similes - A simile is when two different things are compared using the word "like" or "as." (EXAMPLE: hot as popping grease, smells like a cow.) Find as many similes as you can in this chapter.

JOURNAL WRITING: Students Write

C Write as many similes as you can.

BRIDGE TO TERABITHIA

CHAPTER 2

VOCABULARY:

C

nauseate	shuddered	genuine	muddled	hypocritical
clamp	discourage	pudgy	scribble	endure
midair	tremble	talented	pandemonium	tilt

PREREADING DISCUSSION:

Ap Have you ever been new to a place? How would you go about introducing yourself? In this chapter, you meet a new character. Let's see how she introduces herself.

POSTREADING DISCUSSION:

K How did Leslie introduce herself? What else could she have done? Why?

An What else could Jess have done? Why?

Ev Did they get off to a good start? Why or why not?

JOURNAL WRITING: Students Write

Ev Write an entry to your diary about their meeting first from Leslie's point of view and then from Jess's point of view.

BRIDGE TO TERABITHIA

CHAPTER 3

VOCABULARY:

 C

fluttered	smirk	conspicuous	ignore	champion
radiator	initial	eliminations	protests	retreat
deliberately	slope	conversation	sarcasm	roused
grudgingly	repulsive	concentrate	conceited	

PREREADING DISCUSSION: Students Write in Journal

Ap Have you ever been in some kind of a contest?

An How did you feel before the contest? During the contest? After the contest? (Students write their feelings in their journals.)

POSTREADING DISCUSSION: Teacher Writes on Board

C How did Jess feel about the contest? (Before, during, and after the contest)

JOURNAL WRITING: Students Write

An How was the way Jess felt about his contest the same as the way you felt about yours? How was it different?

CHAPTER 4

VOCABULARY:

 C

suspense	suburban	coward	contempt	falter
intoxicated	consolation	gymnastics	columns	abrupt
consolidated	upheaval	vigorously	melodic	ominously
gorgeous	rumpus	solemn	gully	sacred

PREREADING DISCUSSION: Students Draw in Journal

Sy Imagine your special place. What would you name it? Draw it in your journal.

POSTREADING DISCUSSION: Teacher Writes on Board

An How is Jess and Leslie's imaginary place the same as and different from yours? List students' responses on the board.

BRIDGE TO TERABITHIA

JOURNAL WRITING: Students Write

`Ev` Write a description of your special imaginary place.

CHAPTER 5

VOCABULARY:

`C`
revenge	composition	tangle	doubtful	stricken
snickered	regicide	nudge	vigorously	parapets

PREREADING DISCUSSION:

`Ap` How can a bully be like a giant? How would you handle a bully?

POSTREADING DISCUSSION: Teacher Writes on Board

`An` What would have happened if Jess had fought Janice?

JOURNAL WRITING: Students Write

`Ev` Write how one of the other plans for dealing with Janice would have worked out.

CHAPTER 6

VOCABULARY:

`C`
obsessed	wicker	gazed	prompt	speculation
desperate	sneer	annoyance	surplus	moping
aisle	collapse	foundling	paralyzed	prescribed

PREREADING DISCUSSION: Students Write in Journal

`Ev` What kinds of gifts would you give Jess if you were Leslie? What kinds of gifts would you give Leslie if you were Jess?

POSTREADING DISCUSSION:

`Ev` What other gifts would have been good to give? Defend your answer.

JOURNAL WRITING: Students Write

`Ev` Write a paragraph in your journal explaining why one of your gift ideas was a good choice.

BRIDGE TO TERABITHIA

CHAPTER 7

VOCABULARY:

reluctant	nuisance	anxiety	betray	fetch
shrug	predator	delicate	exile	tolerate
alcove	realm	canker	sore	dumbfounded

PREREADING DISCUSSION:

Have you ever had someone find out about a secret you had? How did it feel? What did you do? In this chapter someone finds out about a secret. Read to see what happens.

POSTREADING DISCUSSION: Teacher Writes on Board

How does Jess feel when May Belle says she followed him? How are your feelings the same as Jess's? (List students' responses.)

JOURNAL WRITING: Students Write

Write a letter to Leslie from Jess stating what happened with May Belle and what you plan to do.

CHAPTER 8

VOCABULARY:

complacent	spectacle	unison	vile
congregation	raveled	rhythmically	garbled
tantrum	weary	sanctuary	decent

PREREADING DISCUSSION:

What do you think will happen in a chapter entitled "Easter"? Students should write one event they think might happen in their journals.

POSTREADING DISCUSSION: Teacher Writes on Board

Have students reconstruct and sequence the events of this chapter (list them on the board).

BRIDGE TO TERABITHIA

JOURNAL WRITING: Students Write

`Ev` How would the chapter have been different if the event you thought might happen had happened?

CHAPTER 9

VOCABULARY:

`C`
mournfully	confine	vanquished	defeat	conspire
momentarily	chariots	repent	peculiar	discern

PREREADING DISCUSSION:

`Ev` What do you do when you have a bad feeling about something? How do you handle it? Jess has a bad feeling. See what he does about it in this chapter.

POSTREADING DISCUSSION: Teacher Reads

Read aloud to the students the passage beginning, "It had seemed to Jess when he went to bed Wednesday night that he could relax...," and ending, "He hardly slept the rest of the night, listening to the horrid rain and knowing that no matter how high the creek came, Leslie would still want to cross it."

`C` How did Jess make himself feel better?

JOURNAL WRITING: Students Write

`Sy` Write a letter to Leslie from Jess explaining how you felt at the end of the chapter.

CHAPTER 10

VOCABULARY:

`C` unemployment   idly   scrawny

POSTREADING DISCUSSION: Students Write in Journal

`Ap` What would a perfect day for Jess involve? (Have the students list these things in their journals.)

PREREADING DISCUSSION: Teacher Writes on Board

`An` How was the day a good day, how was it a bad day? (List events on the board.)

BRIDGE TO TERABITHIA

JOURNAL WRITING: Students Write

`C` How many of the elements in Jess's perfect day did you think would have occurred in this chapter?

CHAPTER 11

VOCABULARY:

`C` | relentlessly   accusation   swerved   doused
lopsided   sensation

PREREADING DISCUSSION:

`Ev` What is it like to have someone or something close to you die? What does it feel like? (Encourage the students to use similes.)

POSTREADING DISCUSSION: Teacher Reads

`Ap` Read aloud to the students the passage beginning, "It came into his mind that someone had told him that Leslie was dead," and ending, "Perhaps they could run over the hill and across the fields to the stream and swing themselves into Terabithia." Discuss students' experiences that are like this.

JOURNAL WRITING: Students Write

`Ap` Write a description of how Terabithia would look at night if Jess could have seen it that way with Leslie.

CHAPTER 12

VOCABULARY:

`C` | smothering   imitate   retrieved

PREREADING DISCUSSION:

`An` Have you ever felt stranded? What does it feel like?

`Ev` How might Jess feel stranded?

POSTREADING DISCUSSION: Teacher Reads

`Ev` Read aloud to the students the passage beginning, "He, Jess, was the only one who really cared for Leslie," and ending, "...she had left him stranded there - like an astronaut wandering about the moon. Alone." How does Jess feel stranded?

BRIDGE TO TERABITHIA

JOURNAL WRITING: Students Write

`Ev` | Write about what you would want to do or say to help Jess right now.

CHAPTER 13

VOCABULARY:

`C` |
| piteously | cardinal | traitorous | despite |
| constricting | leisurely | despise | wreath |

PREREADING DISCUSSION:

`C` | Discuss how Jess and May Belle's relationship has grown.

`Ap` | Have students pair up and practice reading Jess and May Belle's dialogue as a play.

`Sy` | Make up a dialogue to reveal the ending of the book.

POSTREADING DISCUSSION: Students Read Play In Pairs; Discussion

Have the students read the dialogue out loud as a play. Begin with May Belle's line, "Help! Jess! Help me!" and end with Jess's line, "Let's go eat."

`C` | Discuss how Jess and May Belle feel about each other.

`Ev` | How do you think Leslie would have felt about May Belle being part of Terabithia?

JOURNAL WRITING: Students Write

`Ap` | Write Jess's last letter to Leslie explaining to her how he has shared Terabithia with May Belle.

BRIDGE TO TERABITHIA

CULMINATING ACTIVITIES

Ev Have students read the titles and the last paragraphs in each chapter of the book. Do any of them foreshadow Leslie's death? How?

STORY FRAME: Discussion; Students Read; Teacher Writes On Board; Students Fill In Story Frames

C Have the students fill in the characters and setting on their story frames. Discuss the plot and then have the students review their chapter fill-in summaries. Ask the class to brainstorm major events in the story (list these on the board). Consolidate statements and ideas until everyone has an understanding of the summary. Then have the students fill in the summary sections of their story frames.

JOURNAL WRITING: Students Write

Ev Students choose one of the following to do as a culminating activity:

•What would have happened if Leslie hadn't died?

•Describe a picture Jess may have drawn for Leslie.

•Write a newspaper article about Leslie's death.

BRIDGE TO TERABITHIA

MATH

MEASUREMENT, GRAPHING:

Have students run their fastest in several heats over varying distances. Determine the time of each runner. Graph the results and determine how fast they were running (distance = rate x time) and calculate how long it would take to run long distances.

SOCIAL STUDIES

MAPPING:

Draw a map of the area Jess and Leslie lived in. Include each of their houses, the school, church, and Terabithia.

SCIENCE

RAIN CALIBRATIONS:

Study how to determine the amount of rainfall and study how streams swell with rain and can become dangerous. Discuss ways Leslie could have safely crossed the water.

FINE ARTS

DRAWING:

Draw with colored pencils pictures that Jess might have drawn.

MUSIC:

Listen to chamber music like Leslie's family did. Sing songs Jess and Leslie may have sung with Miss Edwards.

PERFORMANCE:

Create and perform a story involving the king and queen of Terabithia.

A WRINKLE IN TIME

CHAPTER 1 — Mrs. Whatsit

C   **1.** What is the setting of this chapter? _____

C   **2.** On another sheet of paper, describe these characters: Meg, Sandy & Dennys, Mother, Charles Wallace, Father, Fortinbras, and Mrs. Whatsit.

An   **3.** How was Charles Wallace different from most children? _____
_____

C   **4.** On another sheet of paper, draw and label a picture of Mrs. Whatsit.

Ap   **5.** What's your recipe for tuna sandwiches? _____
_____

An   **6.** Which character in this chapter is most like you? Why? _____
_____

Ev   **7.** Why do you think the chapter was called "Mrs. Whatsit"? _____
_____

Sy   **8.** What other name would you give this chapter? Why? _____
_____

An   **9.** On another sheet of paper, summarize the plot of this chapter.

A WRINKLE IN TIME

CHAPTER 2 — Mrs. Who

C   **10.** What did Mrs. Murray mean, "You don't have to understand things for them to be"? _____

C   **11.** What do you know about Meg's father? _____

Ev   **12.** If you were Meg, how would you have handled Mr. Jenkin, the principal, differently? _____

An   **13.** How are Calvin and Charles Wallace alike and different? _____ _____

Ap   **14.** Draw Mrs. Who the way she appeared when you first meet her in the chapter.

C   **15.** Describe Mrs. Who. _____

Ev   **16.** Why do you think the chapter was called "Mrs. Who"? _____

Sy   **17.** What other name would you give this chapter? Why? _____

An   **18.** On another sheet of paper, summarize the plot of this chapter.

A WRINKLE IN TIME

CHAPTER 3 — Mrs. Which

K **19.** What subject is Meg very good at? _____

K **20.** Who wrote James Boswell's *Life of Johnson*, New American Library?_____
_____

C **21.** What did Calvin mean when he said, "I can function at the same level as everybody else, I can hold myself down, but it isn't me"? _____
_____

K **22.** Write all you know about Meg's father now. _____
_____
_____

K **23.** What is Meg's biggest worry about her father? _____
_____

Ap **24.** Draw as much of Mrs. Which as she was able to materialize.

Ap **25.** Practice talking like Mrs. Which.

Ev **26.** What kind of feeling did you get when Mrs. Which first spoke? Why? _____
_____
_____

Ev **27.** Why do you think the chapter was called "Mrs. Which"? _____
_____
_____

Sy **28.** What other name would you give this chapter? Why? _____
_____

CHAPTER 4 — The Black Thing

C **29.** On another sheet of paper, draw and label a picture of what Mrs. Which looked like when she materialized.

C **30.** How does each of these characters communicate?

Mrs. Whatsit: _____

Mrs. Who: _____

Mrs. Which: _____

An **31.** What was the same about Mrs. Whatsit before and after she metamorphosed? What had changed? _____

_____

_____

_____

Ev **32.** What do you think were the most important things about Mrs. Whatsit?_____

_____

_____

_____

Ev **33.** Why do you think the chapter was called "The Black Thing"? _____

_____

_____

Sy **34.** What other name would you give this chapter? Why? _____

_____

_____

An **35.** On another sheet of paper, summarize the plot of this chapter.

CHAPTER 5 — The Tesseract

C 36. Explain what the author meant when she wrote, "Mrs. Whatsit was not speaking aloud, and yet through the wings Meg understood words."

_____

_____

_____

_____

Ev 37. When have you understood someone's meaning without words? Explain.

_____

_____

_____

Ev 38. If you could "tesser" where would you go and what would you do?_____

_____

An 39. What kinds of things do you think you could do in a two dimensional world?

_____

C 40. What did Mrs. Whatsit mean, "We can't take credit for our talents, it's how we use them that counts"? _____

_____

Ev 41. On another sheet of paper, write a paragraph about your talents and how you use them.

Ap 42. What other people here on earth do you think are (or were) fighters of the Black Thing? _____

_____

Ev 43. Why do you think the chapter was called "The Tesseract"? _____

_____

Sy 44. What other name would you give this chapter? Why? _____

_____

An 45. On another sheet of paper, summarize the plot of this chapter.

CHAPTER 6 — The Happy Medium

Ev **46.** Why do you think the medium was called the "happy medium"? _____

_____

_____

Ev **47.** Do you agree with what the medium meant when she said, "It's my worst trouble, getting fond. If I didn't get fond I could be happy all the time." Explain on another sheet of paper.

K **48.** Fill in the blanks with the gifts each child received.

Calvin: _____

Meg: _____

Charles: _____

C **49.** What did Mrs. Whatsit mean when she told Charles, "Beware of pride and arrogance, for they may betray you"? Explain on another sheet of paper.

Ev **50.** What gifts or advice would you give each character and why?

Meg: _____

_____

Calvin: _____

_____

Charles: _____

_____

Ev **51.** Why do you think this chapter was called "The Happy Medium"? _____

_____

_____

Sy **52.** What other names would you give this chapter? Why? _____

_____

_____

An **53.** On another sheet of paper, summarize the plot of this chapter.

CHAPTER 7 — The Man With Red Eyes

C 54. Draw the long room with machines and what the children found at the end of it.

Ev 55. Why do you think IT wanted Charles so much? _____

_____

C 56. What did it mean, "Meg did not tell the man that patience was not one of her virtues"?_____

_____

_____

Ev 57. Would you have eaten the turkey dinner? Why or why not?_____

_____

Ev 58. What would you have done to keep your mind from being taken over by IT?

_____

_____

C 59. What did the man with the red eyes mean when he said to Charles, "I am peace and utter rest. I am freedom from all responsibility. To come in to me is the last difficult decision you need to make"?_____

_____

_____

An 60. Wax eloquent in your description of how the man with the red eyes is like Darth Vader in *Star Wars*.

Ev 61. Why do you think the chapter was called "The Man With Red Eyes"?_____

_____

Sy 62. What other name would you give this chapter? Why? _____

_____

An 63. On another sheet of paper, summarize the plot of this chapter.

CHAPTER 8 — The Transparent Column

Ap **64.** Practice walking like Charles Wallace in this chapter.

An **65.** In Charles Wallace's mind, how is IT like a father? _____

_____

_____

K **66.** What happens to those who get sick on Camazotz? _____

_____

Ev **67.** Explain how you think IT puts people to sleep? _____

_____

_____

C **68.** What did Meg mean, "Maybe I don't like being different, but I don't want to be like everyone else either"? _____

_____

Ev **69.** How do you think Meg would change herself if she could? _____

_____

_____

C **70.** What does the sentence, "IT sometimes calls ITself the Happiest Sadist," mean?_____

_____

Ev **71.** Why do you think IT didn't annihilate the little boy who didn't bounce the ball properly? _____

_____

Ev **72.** Why do you think the chapter was called "The Transparent Column"? _____

_____

Sy **73.** What other name would you give this chapter? Why?_____

_____

_____

An **74.** On another sheet of paper, summarize the plot of this chapter.

A WRINKLE IN TIME

CHAPTER 9 — IT

C 75. Draw Meg's father in the transparent column.

An 76. How was Charles and Meg's father like the Shakespearian character who was "confined into a cloven pine"? _____

_____

_____

Sy 77. From the father's point of view, write your reaction to seeing your daughter and son after such a long separation. _____

_____

_____

_____

C 78. Draw IT.

C 79. What did Meg mean when she said, "...like and equal are not the same thing"?

_____

_____

_____

CHAPTER 10 — Absolute Zero

C   **80.** What did Meg's father mean, "I had almost come to the conclusion that I was wrong to fight, that IT was right after all"?_____

_____

_____

Ap **81.** Explain a time when you have felt the same way as Meg's father, that it was wrong to fight. _____

_____

_____

_____

Ev **82.** What do you think happened to Hank? _____

_____

_____

C   **83.** What did it mean to Meg when, "Disappointment was as dark and corrosive in her as the Black Thing"? _____

_____

_____

C   **84.** Draw and label all parts of the creature.

Ev **85.** How would you have felt if you were Meg and were picked up by the creature? _____

_____

Ev **86.** Why do you think the chapter was called "Absolute Zero"?_____

_____

_____

Sy **87.** What other name would you give this chapter? Why? _____

_____

_____

An **88.** On another sheet of paper, summarize the plot of this chapter.

A WRINKLE IN TIME

CHAPTER 11 — Aunt Beast

An   **89.** How do you think Meg's pain is like having your arm or leg fall asleep? _____

_____

_____

Sy   **90.** How would you explain vision, light, and dark to someone who can't see?

_____

_____

_____

An   **91.** How was Aunt Beast's world of darkness different from the Black Thing's?

_____

_____

Sy   **92.** What different name would you give Aunt Beast? Why? _____

_____

_____

C   **93.** What did the author mean about Meg: "It was she who was limited by her senses, not the blind beasts"? _____

_____

_____

Sy   **94.** How would you describe Mrs. Whatsit, Mrs. Who, and Mrs. Which so the blind beasts would understand. _____

_____

_____

Ev   **95.** Why do you think the chapter was called "Aunt Beast"? _____

_____

_____

Sy   **96.** What other name would you give this chapter? Why? _____

_____

_____

A WRINKLE IN TIME

CHAPTER 12 — The Foolish and the Weak

C   **97.** What did Mrs. Whatsit mean when she told Meg, "We want nothing from you that you do without grace"? _____

_____

Ev   **98.** If you were Meg would you go back to Camazotz? Why or why not? _____

_____

K   **99.** What were the gifts that each of these characters gave Meg?

Mrs. Whatsit: _____

Mrs. Who: _____

Mrs. Which: _____

C   **100.** What did the author mean when she described Charles, "...with a tic in his forehead reiterating the revolting rhythm of IT"? _____

_____

_____

K   **101.** What did Meg have that IT didn't have? _____

_____

Ev   **102.** What other feelings do you think Meg had that IT didn't have? _____

_____

An   **103.** On another sheet of paper, tell how you and Meg are alike.

Ev   **104.** Why do you think this chapter was called "The Foolish and the Weak"? ____

_____

_____

Sy   **105.** What other name would you give this chapter? Why? _____

_____

_____

An   **106.** On another sheet of paper, summarize the plot of this chapter.

© 1990 by Incentive Publications, Inc., Nashville, TN.

A WRINKLE IN TIME

1. Construct a model of Camazotz and label everything. Tell what events of the book happened there.

2. Make a detailed picture book of all the places Meg, Calvin, and Charles traveled and label each picture.

3. Write a story or act out a play about how the Earth gets rid of the shadow of the Black Thing forever.

4. Dress up like one of the characters and explain what happened to you during the book and afterward.

5. Devise a diorama showing one part of the story. Be prepared to explain it.

6. Tape-record a play about a part of the book or what happened after all the characters got home.

7. Describe the typical day of a person on Camazotz.

8. Write or tell about Meg from Aunt Beast's point of view.

9. Make a model of Aunt Beast and explain her part of the book.

© 1990 by Incentive Publications, Inc., Nashville, TN.

A WRINKLE IN TIME

PRELIMINARY ACTIVITIES

GETTING READY TO READ:

K | Who is the author? *Madeleine L'Engle*

K | Has the book won any awards? *Newbery Medal*

K | What other books has the author written? *A Wind in the Door, A Swiftly Tilting Planet*

K | To whom is the book dedicated? *Charles Wadsworth Camp and Wallace Collin Franklin*

Ap | What do you think a "wrinkle in time" is?

An | Where do you think the story takes place?

An | How many characters might it have?

An | What do you think the story is about?

PREREADING DISCUSSION:

An | Have you ever felt "out of sorts" with everyone - that you are different and can't really communicate with anyone? How did it feel? (List the students' responses on the board.)

Ap | Who was the one person or thing you could talk to that would understand you?

The main character of this book feels "out of sorts," too. See who her special person is.

JOURNAL WRITING: Students Write

Sy | Describe the special person you can talk to in your life. What do you talk about? How does that person help you?

CHAPTER 1

VOCABULARY:

C |

frenzied	luxurious	preliminaries	exclusive	tesseract
crevices	delinquent	diction	liniment	serenity
subside	impressive	supine	gossip	vulnerable
prodigious	agile			

A WRINKLE IN TIME

PREREADING DISCUSSION: Teacher Writes on Board

Ev | A strange mood is going to be set at the beginning of this book. How do you think the author might do that? If you were writing a story, what could you do to set the mood?

POSTREADING DISCUSSION:

Read aloud to the students the section beginning, "It was a dark and stormy night," and ending, "It's a privilege, not a punishment."

An | How is the weather like Meg's life?

Ev | How would the mood have been different if it were a beautiful, sunny day?

JOURNAL WRITING: Students Write

Sy | Think about your own mood right now. Write a paragraph describing a scene outside that would reveal your mood.

CHAPTER 2

VOCABULARY:

C |
unceremoniously	belligerent	peremptory	physicist	dilapidated
moron	antagonistic	assimilate	placid	sarcastic
inadvertently	tractable	ferocious		

PREREADING DISCUSSION:

Ap | Have you ever had feelings that you couldn't understand? Give examples of these feelings. In this chapter different characters talk about their feelings. See if any of them felt the way you did.

POSTREADING DISCUSSION: Teacher Writes on Board

C | What characters in the story had feelings they didn't understand? (Teacher lists on the board characters and their feelings.)

C | Find passages in the chapter where each character tries to explain his or her feelings.

An | How are their feelings similar to those you've had?

A WRINKLE IN TIME

JOURNAL WRITING: Students Write

Sy | Pretend you are Meg and write a letter to your father. Try to explain your feelings about all that is happening.

CHAPTER 3

VOCABULARY:

C |
| decipher | plaintive | somber | dubious | paltry |
| judicious | tangible | morass | indignant | contradicted |

PREREADING DISCUSSION:

Ev | What are some things that you do really well but don't let anyone know? Meg has something that she does well but hasn't let anyone at school know about it.

POSTREADING DISCUSSION: Teacher Writes on Board

Read aloud to your students the section beginning, "By what countries is Peru bounded," and ending, "I'm all confused again."

C | Discuss what Calvin means when he says that people like him for the most unimportant reasons.

An | What are some important and unimportant reasons to like someone? (Write responses on the board.)

JOURNAL WRITING: Students Write

An | List the important and unimportant reasons people like you.

CHAPTER 4

VOCABULARY:

C |
authoritative	ineffable	clamber	resonant	corporeal
askew	serene	dwindle	elliptic	ephemeral
monoliths	unobscured	inexorable	anguish	metamorphose

PREREADING DISCUSSION: Teacher Writes on Board

Sy | What different forms can evil take? What can it look like, and what does it feel like? (List these on the board.) The characters encounter something evil in this chapter. See what form it takes.

A WRINKLE IN TIME

POSTREADING DISCUSSION:

 Even though the Black Thing wasn't described, what do you feel about it? What kind of evil do you think it can do? Do you think Meg's father is fighting it? How do you know?

JOURNAL WRITING: Students Write

 How is your feeling about the Black Thing different from your feelings about Mrs. Which even though she, too, was in black?

CHAPTER 5

VOCABULARY:

C	dimension	subside	dissolution	curtsied
	intolerable	medium	frantic	severe

PREREADING DISCUSSION: Teacher Writes on Board

Ev Do you think The Black Thing could be influencing things here on Earth? Give your reasons and examples why or why not. (List responses on the board.) See what else the Black Thing might control in this chapter.

POSTREADING DISCUSSION:

Ev How have some people fought the Black Thing here on Earth? What are some other ways to fight it?

JOURNAL WRITING: Students Write

 In your own way how would you fight the Black Thing? Be realistic.

CHAPTER 6

VOCABULARY:

C	unkempt	talisman	myopic	reluctant	precipitous
	aberration	malignant	resilience	propitious	sputtering

PREREADING DISCUSSION: Teacher Writes on Board

An What are the advantages and disadvantages to everyone living in the same kind of house and doing the same kinds of things all at the same time. (List students' responses on the board.) In this chapter you'll see what such a situation is like.

A WRINKLE IN TIME

POSTREADING DISCUSSION: Teacher Writes on Board

 How is Camazotz similar to your hometown? How is it different? (List responses on the board.)

JOURNAL WRITING: Teacher Reads; Students Write

Read aloud to the students the section beginning, "Again they focused their eyes on the crystal ball," and ending with, "But it lost its life in the winning."

 Have the students pretend they are the stars, write what it is like to be a star. What are its feelings? Why does it want to fight the Black Thing? Have them explain their victory over the Black Thing.

CHAPTER 7

VOCABULARY:

latch	nondescript	tolerant	oblique	bilious
bravado	insistently	bland	divert	threshold
perspective	involuntary	opaque	tenacity	insubstantial
remote	preliminary	dilated	belligerent	

PREREADING DISCUSSION: Teacher Writes on Board

Ev What's good about giving someone else all your pain and responsibility? How is it bad? (Teacher lists students' responses on the board.) See how the characters in this chapter react.

POSTREADING DISCUSSION:

Ev What do you think the man with the red eyes gets if you give in to him? Why does he want to "assume all the pain, all the responsibility, all the burdens of thought and decision"? What could you accomplish in your life if you gave in to him?

JOURNAL WRITING: Students write

Ev What will Charles' future be if he stays under the control of the man with the red eyes? What do you think his future would have been if he hadn't been lost?

A WRINKLE IN TIME

CHAPTER 8

VOCABULARY:

 C

transparent	connotations	enlightened	deviate	sulphurous
hysterical	grimace	pedantic	ominous	spindly
somber	defiant	annihilate	pinioned	marionette
sadist	emanate			

PREREADING DISCUSSION: Teacher Writes on Board

 An How do people with differences create problems? How do they solve problems? In this chapter, Charles tries to explain to Meg and Calvin how giving in to IT is better than any other way of living. See if you agree.

POSTREADING DISCUSSION:

 Ev What other ways do you think IT deals with people who have differences? Why do you think differences are so threatening to IT?

JOURNAL WRITING: Students Write

 Sy Write a letter to a friend from IT's point of view convincing your friend of all the good things you (as IT) can do.

CHAPTER 9

VOCABULARY:

 C

imprisoned	brusque	gait	disembodied	revelation
sinister	translucent	formaldehyde	repellent	despite
impenetrable	dais	nauseating	loathing	endurance
insolent	omnipotent	miasma	revulsion	

PREREADING DISCUSSION: Students Write in Journal

 Ap What are some of your faults? (After discussion students list their faults in their journals.) Remember Mrs. Whatsit gave Meg her faults to help her rescue her father? See what she does with them and how they are similar to and different from yours.

A WRINKLE IN TIME

POSTREADING DISCUSSION:

An | How did Meg's faults help her to rescue her father?

JOURNAL WRITING: Students Write

Sy | How would your faults have helped rescue Meg's father?

CHAPTER 10

VOCABULARY:

C |

consciousness	devoured	atrophied	indentations	inverted
assuaged	illusion	haunches	corrosive	fallible

PREREADING DISCUSSION:

An | How do you want your parents or the adults around you to be? How do you want them to be strong, to be fallible? How do you want them to handle things? Meg has definite expectations about how she wants things to be now that her father has been found. Read to see what her expectations are.

POSTREADING DISCUSSION: Teacher Reads

Read aloud to the students the passage beginning, "She had found her father and he had not made everything all right," and ending with, "And we know that all things work together for good to them that love God, to them who are called according to His purpose."

An | How did Meg want her father to be like IT?

JOURNAL WRITING: Students Write

Sy | Write a letter to Meg from her father's point of view explaining why he cannot be like IT.

CHAPTER 11

VOCABULARY:

C |

emanate	pungent	temporal	virtue	trepidation
exert	converge	absurd	acute	perplex
despondency	frigid	reverberate	indescribable	distraught

A WRINKLE IN TIME

PREREADING DISCUSSION: Teacher Writes on Board

`An` What beautiful, or lovely, or good things can you see and which ones can you feel? (Write students' responses on the board.) Read to find out which good things in this chapter are seen and which are felt.

POSTREADING DISCUSSION:

`Ap` What kinds of things are the creatures missing out on because they can't see? What kinds of feelings do you have that they have? What are some ways of demonstrating your feelings about someone without doing something visible?

JOURNAL WRITING: Students Write

`Ap` Who is like Aunt Beast in your life? How?

CHAPTER 12

VOCABULARY:

`C`
accord	permeate	vulnerable	appalling
contagious	dwindled	unadulterated	exuberance
vestige	imperceptibly	inexorable	

PREREADING DISCUSSION: Teacher Writes on Board

`An` Think of all the adjectives (descriptive words) that you think IT is and IT is not. In this chapter Meg is told she has something that IT does not. Read to find out what it is.

POSTREADING DISCUSSION:

`Ev` What kinds of things can love overcome? How?

`An` Does love seem to be the missing ingredient in all bad and evil things?

`Ev` Who in your life or in the world could you save with your love?

JOURNAL WRITING: Students Write

`Sy` What situations in the world (or in your life) could be changed by love? Explain how.

A WRINKLE IN TIME

CULMINATING ACTIVITIES

POSTREADING DISCUSSION:

 What was your favorite part of the book? What was your least favorite part? Why?

 Where do you think Mrs. Whatsit, Mrs. Who, and Mrs. Which were heading at the end of the book?

STORY FRAME: Discussion; Students Read; Teacher Writes On Board; Students Fill In Story Frames

 Have the students fill in the characters and setting on their story frames. Discuss the plot and then have the students review their chapter fill-in summaries. Ask the class to brainstorm major events in the story (list these on the board). Consolidate statements and ideas until everyone has an understanding of the summary. Then have the students fill in the summary sections of their story frames.

JOURNAL WRITING: Students Write

 Students choose one of the following to write as a culminating activity:

• Make up a dialogue between Charles Wallace and the teacher on his first day in school.

• Explain how Meg's life had changed after she rescued her father and Charles.

• What happened to Calvin?

• What problems will Charles face in his life? What will he become?

• Write a newspaper account of how Mr. Murray got back home.

A WRINKLE IN TIME

MATH

MODELS:

Discuss, draw, and construct models of one-dimensional, two-dimensional, and three-dimensional shapes. Discuss, then, what the fourth and fifth dimensions might be.

SOCIAL STUDIES

COMPARATIVE FREEDOMS/RIGHTS:

In groups, write up a charter or constitution about everyone's rights in your class and on Camazotz. Compare them and give reasons about each being right.

SCIENCE

SENSING, FEELING, SEEING:

Blindfold students and have them experience things that can't be seen. Have them go on a "trust walk" where they are blindfolded and their partner is not.

FINE ARTS

IMPRESSIONISTIC COLLAGE/DRAWINGS:

Make a collage or drawings of Aunt Beast's planet that show the "seeing" part and the "feeling" part of it.

Island Of The Blue Dolphins

ISLAND OF THE BLUE DOLPHINS

CHAPTER 1

C   **1.** On another piece of paper, describe Karana and her family.

C   **2.** Explain how Ramo was "quick as a cricket." _____

_____

C   **3.** Explain Ramo's statement that the sea "...is a flat stone without any scratches." _____

_____

C   **4.** What do you think the small cloud sitting on the stone was? Why? _____

_____

Ap   **5.** What would you have done if you had seen the ship? Why?_____

_____

Ap   **6.** The Russian stood with his feet set apart and his fists on his hips. How did he feel?_____

_____

Ev   **7.** Why do you think Chief Chowig gave his real name to the Aleuts? _____

_____

C   **8.** What is the problem in this chapter? _____

An   **9.** On another piece of paper, write the three main events of this chapter.

CHAPTER 2

C   **10.** On another piece of paper, draw a picture of the island. Label spots discussed in the book.

C   **11.** What "good fortune" befell the tribe? _____

K   **12.** What did the Aleuts ask for? _____

C   **13.** Explain what it means, "The Aleut grunted to his companion." _____

Ev   **14.** Do you think it was right to spy on the Aleuts? _____

Ev   **15.** What do you think the trouble will be? Explain. _____

_____

An   **16.** On another piece of paper, write the three main events of this chapter.

ISLAND OF THE BLUE DOLPHINS   Individual Learning Unit Cont.

CHAPTER 3

An   **17.** How is an otter different from a seal? _____

_____

K   **18.** How did many of the tribe feel about the killing of the otters? _____

_____

K   **19.** How did Karana feel about the killing? Why? _____

_____

C   **20.** List signs that show the Aleuts were readying to leave. _____

_____

C   **21.** What was the question everyone had? _____

Ev   **22.** What do you think Captain Orlov will do? Why? _____

_____

Sy   **23.** What title would you give this chapter? Why? _____

_____

An   **24.** On another piece of paper, write the three main events of this chapter.

CHAPTER 4

An   **25.** What feeling do you get from the first paragraph of this chapter? Why?_____

_____

C   **26.** What happened to cause the battle? _____

Ev   **27.** What do you think could have been done to prevent it? _____

Ev   **28.** Do you think Captain Orlov had more chests of beads on the boat? Why?___

_____

K   **29.** What did Karana think caused the death of her father? _____

Sy   **30.** What title would you give this chapter? Why? _____

_____

An   **31.** On another piece of paper, write the three main events of this chapter.

CHAPTER 5

C 32. Explain what it means, "There was no woman who had not lost a father or a husband, a brother or a son"? _____

_____

C 33. Explain, "Most of those who snared fowl and found fish in the deep water and built canoes are gone." _____

_____

An 34. What do you think the men's opinion was when the women did their work? What were the women's reasons?_____

_____

C 35. Explain, "Those who had died at Coral Cave were still with us." _____

_____

Ap 36. What other decision could Kimki have made? _____

Ev 37. Explain what you think will happen to Kimki._____

_____

Sy 38. What title would you give this chapter? Why? _____

_____

An 39. On another piece of paper, write the three main events of this chapter.

CHAPTER 6

C 40. Explain, "...fog shrouded the island." _____

_____

K 41. Why was the tribe concerned about the Aleuts? _____

_____

K 42. What was their plan to flee? _____

An 43. What were the similarities between the Aleut ship and the new ship? What were the differences? _____

Ev 44. Why do you think Kimki did not return with the ship? _____

Sy 45. What title would you give this chapter? Why? _____

An 46. On another piece of paper, write the three main events of this chapter.

ISLAND OF THE BLUE DOLPHINS   Individual Learning Unit Cont.

CHAPTER 7

Ap 47. Draw a face with the markings Ulape put on herself.

C 48. Explain, "The boat pitched so wildly that in one breath you could see the ship and in the next breath it had gone." _____

_____

_____

An 49. List reasons for Karana to stay on the ship and reasons for her to jump overboard._____

_____

Sy 50. What title would you give this chapter? Why? _____

_____

An 51. On another piece of paper, write the three main events of this chapter.

CHAPTER 8

C 52. Explain, "The huts looked like ghosts in the cold light." _____

_____

An 53. Why did Ramo say he didn't care whether or not the ship came back?

_____

Ap 54. "Ramo threw out his chest." Do this. How do you think he is feeling?_____

_____

An 55. List some of the ways you think Karana needed Ramo's help._____

_____

C 56. How do you know Ramo put up a fight before he died? _____

_____

Ev 57. What would you do about the dogs if you were Karana?_____

_____

Sy 58. What title would you give this chapter? Why? _____

_____

An 59. On another piece of paper, write the three main events of this chapter.

ISLAND OF THE BLUE DOLPHINS   Individual Learning Unit Cont.

CHAPTER 9

Ev   60. Why do you think Karana decided to move away from the village? _____

_____

C   61. Why were no weapons left behind by the tribe? _____

_____

An   62. List reasons for Karana to keep the trinkets and reasons to throw them away.

_____

_____

C   63. This chapter involved many decisions Karana made. List them.

_____

_____

_____

Sy   64. What title would you give this chapter? Why? _____

_____

An   65. On another piece of paper, write the three main events of this chapter.

CHAPTER 10

Sy   66. Describe what you think one of Karana's dreams might be. _____

_____

An   67. Pretend you are Karana and list your reasons for staying on the island and for leaving it. _____

_____

_____

Ev   68. Why do you think dolphins are a good omen? _____

_____

Sy   69. What title would you give this chapter? Why? _____

_____

An   70. On another piece of paper, write the three main events of this chapter.

ISLAND OF THE BLUE DOLPHINS Individual Learning Unit Cont.

CHAPTER 11

K 71. List the things that filled Karana with happiness.

_____

_____

_____

Ev 72. Explain her statement, "Now I knew I would never go again." Why do think she feels that way? _____

_____

C 73. What did Karana look for when searching for a site to build her new home?

_____

_____

Sy 74. What title would you give this chapter? Why? _____

_____

_____

An 75. On another piece of paper, write the three main events of this chapter.

CHAPTER 12

Ap 76. Draw a picture and label the shelter Karana built.

K 77. What were sai-sai and what were they used for? _____

_____

K 78. What was Karana's concern at the end of the chapter? _____

_____

Ev 79. Do you think she will accomplish it? Why or why not? _____

_____

Sy 80. What title would you give this chapter? Why? _____

_____

_____

An 81. On another piece of paper, write the three main events of this chapter.

ISLAND OF THE BLUE DOLPHINS   Individual Learning Unit Cont.

CHAPTER 13

Ap   **82.** Draw this scene: "Like gray boulders the bulls sat on the pebbly slope."

An   **83.** How are sea elephant babies the same as and different from human babies?

_____

C   **84.** Explain, "It was better not to put them on their guard." _____

_____

C   **85.** Explain, "Quickly he overtook his rival and with a single thrust of the shoulders overturned him." _____

_____

C   **86.** Explain, "...the old bull whirled around and turned upon his pursuer." _____

_____

Ev   **87.** What do you think will happen in the next chapter? _____

_____

Sy   **88.** What title would you give this chapter? Why? _____

_____

An   **89.** On another piece of paper, write the three main events of this chapter.

CHAPTER 14

Ev   **90.** What do you think happened to Karana's leg? _____

_____

C   **91.** Explain, "...the wild dogs were stalking around the brush until morning but not venturing close." _____

_____

Ap   **92.** Draw some of the pictures Karana's ancestors may have made in the cave.

An   **93.** How do you think Karana felt at the end of the chapter? Why? _____

_____

Sy   **94.** What title would you give this chapter? Why? _____

_____

An   **95.** On another piece of paper, write the three main events of this chapter.

ISLAND OF THE BLUE DOLPHINS Individual Learning Unit Cont.

CHAPTER 15

Ev 96. What do you think would have happened if Karana had taken one of the pups? Why? _____

_____

Ev 97. Why do you think Karana didn't kill the leader of the dogs but instead brought him home with her? _____

_____

C 98. Explain, "I had no thought he would live and I did not care." _____

_____

C 99. Why didn't Karana sleep in her house the first four nights?_____

_____

Ap 100. What name would you give the dog and why? _____

_____

Sy 101. What title would you give this chapter? Why? _____

_____

An 102. On another piece of paper, write the three main events of this chapter.

CHAPTER 16

C 103. Explain, "Tell me why it is that you are such a handsome dog and yet such a thief." _____

_____

C 104. Why was Karana no longer lonely? _____

_____

C 105. What is a devil-fish? _____

An 106. How is a devil-fish the same as other fish? How is it different? Explain on a separate sheet of paper.

Sy 107. What title would you give this chapter? Why? _____

_____

An 108. On another piece of paper, write the three main events of this chapter.

ISLAND OF THE BLUE DOLPHINS Individual Learning Unit Cont.

CHAPTER 17

C   **109.** On another piece of paper, draw the spear Karana made.

C   **110.** Explain, "The wild dogs had been to the house many times that winter and he paid no heed to them." _____

_____

Ev   **111.** Would you have stopped the fight? Why or why not? _____

_____

C   **112.** What does it mean that Rontu's howl, "...was the sound of many things that I did not understand"? _____

_____

Ap   **113.** Why do you think the wild dogs divided into two packs? _____

_____

Sy   **114.** What title would you give this chapter? Why? _____

_____

An   **115.** On another piece of paper, write the three main events of this chapter.

CHAPTER 18

C   **116.** On another piece of paper, draw the scene described in the first chapter.

C   **117.** List the types of birds mentioned in this chapter. _____

_____

Ap   **118.** What name would you rather have been called? Why? _____

_____

C   **119.** Explain, "...all the women of our tribe had singed their hair as a sign of mourning." _____

_____

Ap   **120.** What do people in your family do when they are mourning? _____

_____

Sy   **121.** What title would you give this chapter? Why? _____

_____

An   **122.** On another piece of paper, write the three main events of this chapter.

ISLAND OF THE BLUE DOLPHINS   Individual Learning Unit Cont.

CHAPTER 19

K 123. On another piece of paper, list all of the sealife mentioned in this chapter.

Ap 124. Draw the eyes of the devil-fish.

C 125. Explain how the devil-fish eyes are like, "...the eyes of a spirit I had once seen on a night that rain fell and lightening forked in the sky." _____

_____

C 126. Explain, "I was suddenly covered, or so it seemed, with a countless number of leeches sucking at my skin." _____

_____

Ev 127. Would you spear another devil-fish if you were Karana? Why or why not? ___

_____

Sy 128. What title would you give this chapter? Why? _____

_____

An 129. On another piece of paper, write the three main events of this chapter.

CHAPTER 20

C 130. Draw the thing Karana made from shells to keep the birds away.

Ap 131. What three things would you do on the island if there was no more work?

    1. _____

    2. _____

    3. _____

An 132. When Rontu's bark echoed through the cave, why did it send a "cold feeling" down Karana's back? _____

_____

C 133. What things did Karana do to not let the Aleuts know she was there?_____

_____

Ev 134. What do you think the Aleuts would do to Karana if they caught her? _____

_____

Sy 135. What other title would you give this chapter? Why? _____

An 136. On another piece of paper, write the three main events of this chapter.

ISLAND OF THE BLUE DOLPHINS Individual Learning Unit Cont.

CHAPTER 21

C **137.** Why was Karana most afraid of the Aleut girl? _____
_____

Ev **138.** Why do you think Karana didn't throw spears at the Aleut girl? _____
_____

C **139.** Why didn't Karana give her name to Tutok? _____
_____

C **140.** On another piece of paper, draw the necklace.

Ev **141.** How do you think Karana will react to the girl? Why? _____
_____

Ev **142.** What gift would you have given her? Why? _____
_____

Sy **143.** What title would you give this chapter? Why? _____
_____

An **144.** On another piece of paper, write the three main events of this chapter.

CHAPTER 22

C **145.** How could you tell Karana's anger toward Tutok was lessening? _____
_____

Ev **146.** Why do you think Karana was ready to be friends with Tutok? _____
_____

Ev **147.** Why do you think Karana gave Tutok her secret name? _____
_____

An **148.** What do you think kept Tutok from visiting Karana before she left? _____
_____

C **149.** Explain, "As I thought of Tutok, the island seemed very quiet." _____
_____

Sy **150.** What title would you give this chapter? Why? _____

An **151.** On another piece of paper, write the three main events of this chapter.

CHAPTER 23

C 152. Explain, "I did not try to treat its wound with herbs because salt water heals and the herbs would have washed off anyway." _____

_____

C 153. Explain how the otters made, "...pain come to my throat because they were gay and sad also." _____

_____

An 154. How were the otters happy and how were they sad? _____

_____

C 155. Why didn't Karana feel as sad when the otter left as when Tutok left? _____

_____

Sy 156. Karana says, "I would make up things to say to her." What things would you make up to say to Tutok? Why? _____

_____

Ev 157. What would have happened if the otter had stayed? _____

_____

Sy 158. What title would you give this chapter? Why? _____

_____

An 159. On another piece of paper, write the three main events of this chapter.

CHAPTER 24

Ev 160. What do you think happened to Ulape? _____

C 161. Why did Karana have to change Mon-a-nee's name? _____

C _____

162. Explain, "...birds and animals are like people... without them the earth would be an unhappy place." _____

An 163. How are birds and animals like people? How are they unlike people? _____

_____

Sy 164. What title would you give this chapter? Why? _____

An 165. On another piece of paper, write the three main events of this chapter.

ISLAND OF THE BLUE DOLPHINS Individual Learning Unit Cont.

CHAPTER 25

K   **166.** Why did the otter leave Coral Cove every year? _____

_____

C   **167.** Explain, "The passing of the moons had come to mean little..." _____

_____

_____

C   **168.** What do you think Karana meant when she picked up Rontu who was very light, "...as if something about him had already gone." _____

_____

_____

Ev   **169.** Why do you think Rontu went back to his old cave? _____

_____

Sy   **170.** What title would you give this chapter? Why? _____

_____

An   **171.** On another piece of paper, write the three main events of this chapter.

CHAPTER 26

Ap   **172.** On another piece of paper, draw a snare you think Karana made.

C   **173.** List the three ways she used to capture the dog she wanted.

     1. _____

     2. _____

     3. _____

C   **174.** Explain, "Often when I watched him chasing gulls on the sandspit or on the reef barking at the otter, I forgot that he was not Rontu." _____

_____

_____

Sy   **175.** What title would you give this chapter? Why? _____

_____

An   **176.** On another piece of paper, write the three main events of this chapter.

ISLAND OF THE BLUE DOLPHINS   Individual Learning Unit Cont.

CHAPTER 27

C   **177.** What was the, "...great white crest moving down upon the island"? _____

_____

C   **178.** Explain, "Slowly the second wave forced the first one backward," and then, "As a victor drags the vanquished, moved in toward the island." _____

_____

_____

C   **179.** On another piece of paper, draw the beach after the large waves.

Sy   **180.** What title would you give this chapter? Why? _____

_____

An   **181.** On another piece of paper, write the three main events of this chapter.

CHAPTER 28

C   **182.** Explain, "Without a canoe to go where I wanted, I felt uneasy." _____

_____

C   **183.** Draw the site of the ship.

C   **184.** Why didn't Karana hide like she did with the Aleuts? _____

_____

Ev   **185.** Who do you think was on the ship and why had they come? _____

_____

An   **186.** How could the saying, "He who hesitates is lost," apply to this chapter? ___

_____

_____

Ap   **187.** Why do you think the ship went away? _____

_____

Sy   **188.** What title would you give this chapter? Why? _____

_____

An   **189.** On another piece of paper, write the three main events of this chapter.

CHAPTER 29

Ev   **190.** Why do you think the ship came back? _____

_____

Ap   **191.** Draw and label Karana's outfit and face paint.

Ev   **192.** Why do you think the white men made a new dress for her? _____

_____

K   **193.** What had happened to the ship that took her people before? _____

_____

An   **194.** What things would you have thought about when you left the island? _____

_____

Sy   **195.** What title would you give this chapter? Why? _____

_____

An   **196.** On another piece of paper, write the three main events of this chapter.

AUTHOR'S NOTE

C   **197.** Why did the author refer to the main character as, "Girl Robinson Crusoe"?

_____

K   **198.** List the facts you know about the real Indian girl.

     1. _____

     2. _____

     3. _____

     4. _____

     5. _____

     6. _____

C   **199.** Explain, "Excavations on the island show that Indians came here from the north long before the Christian era." _____

C   **200.** Explain about San Nicolas island, "Scientists predict that because of the pounding waves and furious winds it will one day be swept back into the sea." _____

_____

ISLAND OF THE BLUE DOLPHINS

1. Make up a detailed map of the island showing where everything is and label it.

2. Bring a collection of shells, feathers, seaweed, bone, etc., that Karana might have had on the island. Label everything and tell how she used it.

3. Make a necklace that Karana could have given to Tutok. Explain how you made it and why (from Karana's point of view).

4. Make a model of a tide pool and label all the sealife in it.

5. Make some of the utensils and weapons Karana made. Explain them.

6. Compare the tools she made with the ones we use today.

7. Make clothing like Karana wore and explain it.

8. Make up your own sign language and try to communicate to people like the real Indian woman did.

9. Put on a skit or a play of Karana killing the devil-fish or some other part of the story.

10. Create wind chimes out of shells like Karana did to keep the birds away from drying meat. Explain how they work.

© 1990 by Incentive Publications, Inc., Nashville, TN.

ISLAND OF THE BLUE DOLPHINS

PRELIMINARY ACTIVITIES

GETTING READY TO READ:

K Who is the author? *Scott O'Dell*

K Has the book won any awards? *Newbery Medal*

K What other books has the author written? *The Black Pearl, Sing Down the Moon, The 290, Zia*

K To whom is the book dedicated? *The Russell Children: Isaac, Dorsa, Clare, Gillian and Felicity, and to Eric, Cherie, and Twinkle*

An Where do you think the story takes place? *answers will vary*

An How many characters might it have? *answers will vary*

An What do you think the story is about? *answers will vary*

PREREADING DISCUSSION:

Ev How would you feel if you had to live alone and take care of yourself? What would you do? How would you get food?

JOURNAL WRITING: Students Write

Sy Write about how you would get food and shelter if you had to live alone without any family or friends around.

CHAPTERS 1 and 2

VOCABULARY:

C

Aleut	ravine	kelp	concealed	mesa	reef
afloat	crouch	parley	cormorant	league	profit
spring	idle	glistening	sparingly	prey	

PREREADING DISCUSSION: Teacher Writes on Board

Ev Discuss what it means to have two names. Is anyone in class known by another name? Is it like being two people?

Sy While you are reading, think of a secret name you would like to have and don't tell anyone.

ISLAND OF THE BLUE DOLPHINS

POSTREADING DISCUSSION:

Ev Do you think it was right for Chief Chowig not to have shared with the Aleuts? Explain why or why not. Might his decision lead to problems later?

JOURNAL WRITING:

Sy Write about your secret name and why you chose it.

CHAPTERS 3 and 4

VOCABULARY:

C
slain	strewn	pelts	carcasses	ledge
retreat	scattered	surged	pursue	ceased

PREREADING DISCUSSION:

Ev If you have made a bargain with somebody, when is it all right not to keep it? Should you always keep a bargain? Captain Orlov makes a bargain with the chief. Read to see what happens.

POSTREADING DISCUSSION: Teacher Reads; Discussion

Read aloud the passage beginning, "My father lay on a bench and the waves were already washing over him." Ask the students to discuss.

Ev What kind of power do you think the Indians attributed to the secret name? When do you think they used it? Why? Do you agree with the Indians that the chief died because he gave out his secret name?

JOURNAL WRITING: Students Write

Ev Rewrite the events of these chapters from Captain Orlov's point of view.

CHAPTERS 5 and 6

VOCABULARY:

C
abound	portioned	launch	abalone	shirkers
mischief	decreed	fowl	shrouded	ponder
stout	scan	flee		

ISLAND OF THE BLUE DOLPHINS

PREREADING DISCUSSION:

Ev | Have you ever lost a family member? How did it feel (or, how do you think it would feel)? Would you want to move away so you weren't reminded of old memories, or would you want to stay where you are? These questions are dealt with in these chapters. Read to see what the Indians do.

POSTREADING DISCUSSION: Teacher Writes on Board

An | How was the tribe's reaction to the white men's ship similar to their reaction to the Aleut ship? How did they react differently? What does each ship represent? List students' responses in two columns on the board.

JOURNAL WRITING: Students Write

Sy | Pretend you are Karana, and write your feelings about leaving your home. In what ways are you happy about the change? In what ways are you frightened?

CHAPTERS 7 and 8

VOCABULARY:

C | pitched   forlorn   beckon   gusts   clutch   gorge
stride   solemn   scurry   mussels   slink   rites

PREREADING DISCUSSION:

An | What would you take with you if you were moving? Why?

Ev | What do you think Karana will take with her? Why? How might Ramo, Karana's brother, be a problem while she is getting things ready to move? See what everyone packs in these chapters and how Ramo becomes a problem.

POSTREADING DISCUSSION: Teacher Reads; Discussion

Read the passage beginning, "I had not gone far along the trail before I began to wonder if I should not let him go to the cliff by himself."

Ev | Was Karana right to make this decision? Why or why not? Who was responsible for Ramo's death? Why?

JOURNAL WRITING: Students Write

Sy | Write a paragraph from Karana's point of view explaining how she feels about her decision.

ISLAND OF THE BLUE DOLPHINS

CHAPTERS 9 and 10

VOCABULARY:

C

vanished	slinking	patient	crevice	trinkets
smother	sinews	pelican	companion	chafing
ancestors	seeping	pursued	idly	omen

PREREADING DISCUSSION:

Ev Now that Karana is all alone, what kinds of things must she do for herself? What kinds of decisions must she make?

POSTREADING DISCUSSION: Teacher Writes on Board

Ev What do you think would have happened if Karana had continued in the canoe? (List students' responses on the board.)

JOURNAL WRITING: Students Write

Sy Write a dialogue between a man in Karana's tribe explaining why she should not make weapons and Karana explaining why she must.

CHAPTERS 11 and 12

VOCABULARY:

C

brackish	clamor	steady	gnaw	utensils
embers	gruel	pebbly	secure	

PREREADING DISCUSSION:

Ev Explain a time when you were happy to be home. What things around your home did you miss? Karana, too, is happy to be home in this chapter. Read to see what she does.

POSTREADING DISCUSSION:

Ev Do you think Karana will accomplish her goal of getting sea elephant teeth? Why or why not? How do you think she might go about doing it? What problems might she encounter?

JOURNAL WRITING: Students Write

Sy Compare Karana's building materials to those from which your house is made. How are they similar? How are they different?

ISLAND OF THE BLUE DOLPHINS

CHAPTERS 13 and 14

VOCABULARY:

forbade	boulders	rival	gash	flank
injured	waddling	stalking	venturing	herbs
surround	basin	fetch	lobe	

PREREADING DISCUSSION:

 Describe a sea elephant - what it looks like, the texture of its skin, etc. (List the students' responses on the board, which they, in turn, copy into their journals.)

POSTREADING DISCUSSION:

 What do you think would have happened if Karana's leg had not healed?

JOURNAL WRITING: Students Write

 Skim chapter 13 for information about sea elephants. Write a short paragraph about what you have learned.

CHAPTERS 15 and 16

VOCABULARY:

slanted	bared	slits	shaft	bindings
abandoned	lapping	labored	roost	devil-fish

PREREADING DISCUSSION:

Ev Do you think that Karana will be able to kill the wild dogs? Why or why not?

POSTREADING DISCUSSION: Students Skim Chapters

C What has occurred since chapter 10 to make Karana happier and not so lonely as she was? (Have the students skim the chapters and report details.)

JOURNAL WRITING: Teacher Reads; Students Write

Read the passage beginning, "The walls were black and smooth and slanted far up over my head."

Sy Have the students imagine this place and write about some of the fish in the water and some of the sounds they would hear.

ISLAND OF THE BLUE DOLPHINS

CHAPTERS 17 and 18

VOCABULARY:

braided	whined	lure	crouching	crevices
haunches	warily	heed	mourning	singed
plentiful	quarrelsome	twine	faggot	
stunted	perching	shreds	muzzles	
lupines	yucca	barbed	foreleg	

PREREADING DISCUSSION:

What would you do if your pet was in a fight? Karana has to try and break up a fight in chapter 17.

POSTREADING DISCUSSION: Teacher Writes on Board

How are the descriptions of spring in chapter 18 similar to spring in your area? How is Karana's response to spring similar to yours? (List students' responses on the board.)

JOURNAL WRITING: Students Write

Write a paragraph describing how to make a flower wreath or chain.

CHAPTERS 19 and 20

VOCABULARY:

amused	sea urchin	entangled	failing	coils	oblong
dodging	scallop	seized	thong	suckers	

PREREADING DISCUSSION:

How might catching a devil-fish be different from catching a regular fish? What problems might Karana have?

POSTREADING DISCUSSION: Teacher Reads; Discussion

Read the passage beginning, "Seeing the sun shining down and the black shadows drifting over the walls...," and ending with, "They were more alive than the eyes of those who live."

What do you think those figures represent? Who might have put them there? What kind of ritual might have been held?

JOURNAL WRITING: Students Write

Pretend you are living on the Island of the Blue Dolphins long ago. Explain what the figures in the black cave are and why they were put there.

ISLAND OF THE BLUE DOLPHINS

CHAPTERS 21 and 22

VOCABULARY:

tangled	fibers	giddy	gestures	pace	shimmered
sprawled	bored	admire	prow	deserted	circlet

PREREADING DISCUSSION:

 How would you go about communicating with someone who does not speak your language? Read to find out how an Aleut girl communicates with Karana.

POSTREADING DISCUSSION: Teacher Writes on Board

 How was Karana's giving her secret name to the Aleut girl the same as her father's giving his secret name to the Aleuts before? How was it different? (List the students' responses on the board.)

 Do you think anything bad will happen to Karana as a result of her giving her secret name? Why or why not?

JOURNAL WRITING: Students Write

 Write all the things Tutok wanted to say to Karana before she left but couldn't.

CHAPTERS 23 and 24

VOCABULARY:

anchor	smelt	reproachfully	teetering
swoop	nuzzle	fledglings	hobble

PREREADING DISCUSSION:

 Do you kill animals? Why or why not? If you were in Karana's situation, would you be able to kill animals? Karana makes a decision about killing animals in these two chapters.

POSTREADING DISCUSSION: Teacher Reads; Discussion

Read aloud the passage beginning, "After that summer, after being friends with Won-a-nee and her young, I never killed another otter."

ISLAND OF THE BLUE DOLPHINS

Ev Do you think that Karana's decision would be different if she had a human friend with her on the island? How? What circumstances might make her change her mind about killing animals?

JOURNAL WRITING: Students Write

Sy Give reasons to kill animals from Karana's point of view. Then give reasons to kill animals from a hunter's point of view. Then give reasons to kill animals from a supermarket's point of view.

CHAPTERS 25 and 26

VOCABULARY:

C quiver   snares   frisked

PREREADING DISCUSSION:

Ev Have you ever lost a pet? What was it like? What is the use of having a pet if it is going to die? Read to find out what Karana does when she loses a pet.

POSTREADING DISCUSSION: Teacher Reads; Discussion

Read aloud the passage beginning, "One summer the otter did not leave, the summer that Rontu died...," and ending with, "The last year I did not count those."

Ev How does Karana feel in this passage? Have you ever felt like that? What do you think would cheer her up?

JOURNAL WRITING: Students Write

Sy Design a tombstone for Rontu. Beside it, write the things you think Rontu-Aru should know about his father.

CHAPTERS 27 and 28

VOCABULARY:

C shields   trickled   shudder   victor
   hasten   whence   vanquished

PREREADING DISCUSSION:

Ev Have you ever been in an earthquake? What was it like? How do you think an earthquake on land would be different from an earthquake at sea?

ISLAND OF THE BLUE DOLPHINS

POSTREADING DISCUSSION: Teacher Writes on Board

An What good and bad experiences has Karana had with ships in the past? (List students' responses on the board in two columns.)

Ev Do you think she was wise to hesitate before going down to the ship? Why or why not? What do you think would have happened had she gotten on the ship?

JOURNAL WRITING: Teacher Reads; Students Write

Read aloud the passage beginning, "Like two giants they crashed against each other."

Sy Write your own description of the earthquake and tidal waves using as many similes as you can.

CHAPTER 29 and AUTHOR'S NOTE

VOCABULARY:

C
schooner	befriended	predict	indebted
restrain	rescue	curator	excavations

PREREADING DISCUSSION:

Ev How do you think the story will end? Why?

POSTREADING DISCUSSION: Teacher Writes on Board

Ev What questions would you want to ask the real Indian girl? (List the students' responses on the board.)

JOURNAL WRITING: Students Write

Sy Choose one of the questions you would want to ask the real Indian girl. Write a paragraph answering it from her point of view.

ISLAND OF THE BLUE DOLPHINS

MATH

ESTIMATING DISTANCES:

Locate the islands off the coast of southern California on a map, and using the scale, estimate the distance to your town and other locations. Then calculate how long it would take to travel from one place to another.

SOCIAL STUDIES

INDIANS:

Study Indians in your geographic location and compare and contrast them with the Pacific Coast Indians in the book.

SCIENCE

SEA ANIMALS:

Study sea animals mentioned in the book and their part in the food chain. Examples: otters, sea elephants, birds, octopuses, abalone, etc.

FINE ARTS

MODEL:

Make models of one of the figures in the black cave.

JEWELRY:

Make a piece of jewelry that Karana may have made and given to Tutok.

NOTES

NOTES